No Minister &
No, Minister

The True Story
of HarbourFest

To Anthony

No Minister &
No, Minister

The True Story
of HarbourFest

by

Mike Rowse

Thanks for your quiet support

Mike Rowse 3.11.09

NO MINISTER & NO, MINISTER:
THE TRUE STORY OF HARBOURFEST
ISBN 978-988-18693-8-8

© 2009 Mike Rowse

Published in Hong Kong by
Treloar Enterprises Company Limited
www.rowse.com.hk

Printed and bound in Hong Kong
First printing 2009

The cartoons on the front and back covers are reproduced with permission of Gavin Coates, the cartoonist and copyright holder. They first appeared in *The Hong Kong Standard* on 24 June 2004 and 18 October 2003, respectively.

Dedicated to the people of Hong Kong, who deserve better governance than they are getting now, and to my former colleagues in InvestHK. Starved of recognition, resources and support, they nonetheless go all out for the city they and I love with all our hearts.

Contents

Introduction

AN OUTBREAK OF Severe Acute Respiratory Syndrome (SARS) in Hong Kong in early 2003 killed almost 300 people in a few short weeks and left hundreds more with long term medical problems. It also had a severe – but fortunately short term – impact on the local economy. A Government campaign to help the community cope with the economic consequences, and then revive the economy, was broadly successful and by the end of the year Hong Kong was steaming ahead in its usual full-throttle way.

But one item within that Economic Relaunch programme became a political hot potato. The controversy led to disciplinary action being taken against the head of a small government department though no Minister was held politically accountable.

In 2007, the civil servant concerned, having been found guilty by an internal disciplinary panel and having suffered a small penalty, took legal action to clear his name. He sought a Judicial Review in the High Court of three decisions against him, one each by the Chief Executive, the Chief Secretary for Administration and the Secretary for the Civil Service. Moreover, the grounds he cited to justify the review were by implication critical of actions and decisions by the Secretary for Justice and the Financial Secretary of the time. In effect, therefore, he was taking on all five of the most senior political leaders, a royal flush of the Administration, so to speak.

Yet not only did the civil servant win the court case (heard in 2008), he kept his job and retired a few months later with honour. And the judge who ruled in his favour was promoted to the Court of Appeal.

These events would have been remarkable enough in any society at any time. It is difficult to think of another community in Asia or even the world where they would be possible. Yet they took place in Hong Kong eleven years after China resumed the exercise of sovereignty over the one-time British Colony. A tribute both to the Central People's Government's respect for Hong Kong's "high degree of autonomy" as promised in the city's constitutional document known as the Basic Law, and to the resilience of the institutions left behind by the British and nurtured meanwhile by Hong Kong citizens. The Common Law system remained firmly in place and all remain equal before the law.

Much has been written elsewhere about the events which formed the backdrop to the Judicial Review and the disciplinary proceedings which preceded it. But a great deal of the material was inaccurate, or at least incomplete: hence my decision to write this book. For I was that civil servant, and it is time for the true story – the complete story – of HarbourFest to be told.

I have not written this book with the intention of absolving myself of all blame for the problems that arose, nor to point the finger at others. Rather, I have sought to set out what I did and didn't do, and why.

More importantly, the case illustrates a significant structural problem that has arisen since the introduction of the system of Ministerial Accountability in 2002. Unless that issue is addressed, there is a risk that there will be further such instances, casting a shadow over the quality of governance in Hong Kong.

Before we begin the story, we should note that while Hong Kong is a major city of some 7 million people, in many ways it seems more like a village. The circle of people holding senior positions in the Government, in political circles, in the professions, in the private sector or even in major social and sporting organisations, is fairly small and there are many overlaps. It would be all too easy to suspect or imply collusion or conspiracy when there is nothing of the sort, only perfectly innocent coincidence.

Political Backdrop

ON 1 JULY 1997, Hong Kong ceased to be administered as a British Colony and became a Special Administrative Region of the People's Republic of China. The negotiations which led to this orderly transfer had taken place between the two countries over a two-year period from 1982 to 1984. The final agreement was set out in a document known as the Joint Declaration, and was registered with the United Nations as an international treaty. The principle underlying it was a formula popularly known as "One Country, Two Systems" which had been devised by China's paramount leader at the time, Deng Xiaoping. The Joint Declaration in turn formed the basis for drafting the mini-constitution of Hong Kong called the Basic Law.

In broad terms, the Basic Law provides that the socialist system prevailing in the Mainland of China would not apply to Hong Kong, which would instead continue with its existing capitalist economic system. The Common Law legal system would continue to apply and Hong Kong would have its own Court of Final Appeal with no recourse to the Mainland courts. The way of life of Hong Kong people (freedom of religion, speech, assembly etc) would continue unchanged.

Instead of a Governor appointed by and indeed sent from the United Kingdom, Hong Kong's government would in future be headed by a Chief Executive who would be a Hong Kong person elected by Hong Kong people and then appointed by the Central Government in Beijing. An individual could serve a maximum of two five-year terms.

The first Chief Executive of the Hong Kong SAR was Tung Chee Hwa, a well-known shipping magnate who had been a member of the Executive Council (Hong Kong's equivalent of the Cabinet) headed by the last British Governor Chris Patten. Throughout his initial term from 1997 to 2002, Tung largely retained the previous system whereby every policy bureau was headed by a senior civil servant.

At the start of his second term on 1 July 2002, Tung introduced a new layer of political appointees who would sit above the civil service. These persons would be called "Secretaries" and would function as his Ministers. All would report directly to him unlike the previous practice where groups of civil servant secretaries were marshalled by two more senior civil servants, the Chief Secretary for Administration (CS) and the Financial Secretary (FS). As the term "Secretary" had previously been used by the most senior civil servants, their titles were changed to "Permanent Secretary" and there would be one or more of them in each policy bureau, all reporting to their respective Minister.

In the interest of continuity and to emphasise the "business as usual" dimension of the handover, Tung had inherited the whole of Patten's final team. However, as time went by there naturally were changes, the first major one being the retirement in 2001 of CS Anson Chan. She was replaced by Donald Tsang who up to that point had been FS. Tung took advantage of the resulting vacancy to bring in an outsider from the business sector, Antony Leung, to be the new FS. Upon introduction of the new Ministerial system, Tung brought in several other outsiders from the private sector. The most durable was Henry Tang whose initial appointment was as Secretary for Commerce, Industry and Technology (SCIT).

Although the post of CS is nominally slightly more senior than that of FS, and Tsang's move was in theory a promotion, it was widely known in political and media circles that Tung favoured Leung. The game plan, as most understood it, was that Tung would serve out his second term and that Leung, by then more experienced in the ways of the Government, would take over as Chief Executive in 2007.

But it was not to be. Leung blotted his copybook in quite spectacular fashion. In early 2003 he bought a new car having already decided that in his budget for the 2003-04 financial year which he was due to deliver a few weeks later he would substantially increase the first registration tax on new vehicles. Although there was no suggestion Leung had done anything improper in buying a new car for private use, he neglected to report the purchase to the Chief Executive in a subsequent cabinet meeting when the subject arose, thereby creating an unfortunate impression. In politics appearance is everything, and Leung was to pay the ultimate price for this lapse later in the year.[1]

Tung did not have the best of luck during his first term due in large part to circumstances beyond his control, but exacerbated by some steps of his own.

The top priority of those early days was to prove to a sceptical world, and indeed to a cautious Hong Kong populace, that this new concept of "One Country, Two Systems" could in fact work. In this cause Tung was largely successful, partly because he was totally trusted by Beijing and partly because he was well-known through the media as a thoroughly capitalist business leader with a wide circle of international friends and properties in the United States: in other words, he was a regular Hong Kong guy.[2]

But if this constitutional issue was handled satisfactorily, Tung had less luck in other areas. On the second day of the new SAR's life, 2 July 1997, the Thai baht was devalued, an event which triggered the Asian Economic Crisis. Over the next two years, the economies in Hong Kong's part of the world were badly hit. Exports fell and unemployment rose. There was bound to be an adverse effect on the local property market, which was in any event overheated, and there was: over the next few years, as the economy slumped, prices of residential and commercial property fell across the board by an average of some 70%, pushing a large part of the middle class into negative equity (i.e. the value of the outstanding mortgage on their property was higher than its current market value).

Unfortunately for Tung, he had made a splash in his 1997 Policy Address (Hong Kong's equivalent of the annual "State of the Union" speech) by pledging to build 85,000 housing units per year. In fact, this was only a restatement of something that had first surfaced in the Patten years – a reference to a plan to provide 425,000 new homes over five years. But because Tung's splash was followed by the nosedive in values, his policy got the blame. Even though an attack by international speculators on the Hong Kong dollar (pegged since 1983 to the US dollar at 7.8:1) was successfully beaten off, the Government's reputation was badly hit.

Finally, there was the matter of Hong Kong's security legislation (known as Article 23, because that was the relevant clause in the Basic Law which obliged Hong Kong to put in place appropriate safeguards in this area). All communities have laws on the subject of subversion, treason, plotting to overthrow the state, etc., but the draft Bill that was brought forward in early 2003 to give effect to the Article 23 obligation was subject to severe criticism as going too far in some areas and constituting an assault on Hong Kong people's freedoms.

At this point, Hong Kong's middle-class rebelled: income under pressure because of the recession, savings savaged by the plunge in asset values, little or no progress in bringing greater democracy, a deadly new virus cutting down the innocent, perceived "dodgy" behaviour by a senior official, and now liberty under threat – small wonder that on 1 July 2003 (a public holiday to mark SAR Establishment Day) an estimated 500,000 people took to the streets to demonstrate their dissatisfaction with the Government. This was by far the biggest protest march since the transition, only ever exceeded by the 1989 marches to express support for the students in Tiananmen Square, one of which drew some one million concerned Hong Kong citizens out of their homes.

Outbreak of SARS

THE STORY OF HARBOURFEST is intimately entwined with the story of what came to be known as Severe Acute Respiratory Syndrome (SARS).

The first case of SARS came to light in Foshan, a city in southern Guangdong, in November 2002; at the time, the disease was referred to as Atypical Pneumonia (AP). By January 2003, the Guangdong health authorities had noted a number of similar cases and issued an alert to health units throughout the province to be on their guard.

In mid-February, alarmed by reports about what was happening in Guangdong, the Hong Kong medical authorities sought clarification, and were advised that there had been 305 AP cases in Guangdong in the previous three months, with five deaths. The Hong Kong media reported that Guangdong housewives had cleared supermarket shelves of vinegar in the belief that, once boiled, its use could help ward off AP.

The trigger for the epidemic that was to strike Hong Kong came on 21 February when a medical doctor from Guangdong checked into a hotel in Waterloo Road, Kowloon then known as the Metropole but since renamed. He was admitted to Kwong Wah Hospital the next day and died in early March.

Matters now escalated rapidly. On 3 March, the first case of a local health care worker coming down with the disease was detected in Ward 8A of the Prince of Wales Hospital (PWH). The next day, a local resident with respiratory symptoms was admitted to the same hospital after visiting a friend at the Metropole Hotel. Two days later a visiting businessman from Hanoi was admitted to Princess Margaret Hospital with essentially the same symptoms, and was dead within the week.

On 10 March, PWH management reported to the Department of Health that there had been an outbreak of the disease among health care workers in Ward 8A. Two days later the Department issued an alert to all private doctors and hospitals to take appropriate infection control measures and to report any confirmed or suspected AP cases. The Department also reported the Ward 8A outbreak to the World Health Organisation (WHO), which promptly issued a global alert about the situation in Hong Kong.

By 14 March, a total of 43 staff in four different hospitals were found to have the disease although no link between them had been established at that time. The next day, the WHO officially named the disease SARS.

The Hong Kong community was by this stage in a state of alarm and confusion. No-one knew where this new deadly disease had come from, how to stop it or when it would end. Even the doctors were getting sick. For weeks on end, the people of Hong Kong would awake each morning knowing there was going to be more bad news but not where it would strike. This feeling of confusion was shared by parts of the Administration. On 25 March, the Secretary for Education and Manpower Arthur Li announced that there was no need to suspend classes, but he reversed himself just two days later and ordered that all education classes cease from 29 March to 6 April (later extended to 21 April). Classes gradually resumed after that time and by 19 May everyone was back in school.

On 31 March the Director of Health Dr Margaret Chan (who went on later to become head of the WHO) exercised statutory powers to require any person who had been in contact with a SARS sufferer to attend medical assessment at a designated clinic on a daily basis for 10 days. She also imposed an Isolation Order on Block E of a housing estate called Amoy Gardens whose residents suffered a particularly high incidence of the disease. All residents were moved out the next day to holiday camps where they were to remain until midnight 9 April. The Amoy Gardens outbreak was to be the subject of a separate inquiry.

On 2 April, the WHO issued a travel advisory against non-essential travel to Hong Kong (the United States Centres for Disease Control and Prevention – known as CDC – issued a similar advisory on 1 May). By this time, the wearing of masks was common in the general community as people sought to protect themselves from the coughs and sneezes of others, and also not to pass on any of their own germs. People were reluctant to touch lift buttons or handrails on buses – anything in fact where others' germs might linger – with their bare hands, preferring to use a tissue. Building managements began to disinfect lift panels every hour.

On 17 April, passengers departing from the airport began to have their body temperature checked, a process extended to arriving passengers a few days later. On 24 April the check was applied to those arriving from Mainland China via the land border at Hung Hom and Lo Wu and extended to all ports and land crossing points two days later.

SARS was largely contained by the middle of the following month and the WHO lifted its general travel advisory on 23 May as the number of new cases had dropped to less than five per day. The disease was finally brought under control in June. There had been a total of 1755 cases, 299 of them fatal. The WHO removed Hong Kong from its list of areas with recent transmission on 23 June and the CDC lifted its travel advisory on 25 June. Hong Kong's pariah status was ended.

But the effects were to linger for some while yet. Various investigations and inquiries on the handling of SARS were launched. The most authoritative of these was conducted by a panel of independent experts co-chaired by Sir Cyril Chantler and Professor Sian Griffiths. The "expert committee" did not find any individual culpable for the Government's handling of the outbreak. Indeed, in their 2 October covering letter to the then Chief Executive C H Tung forwarding the final report the co-chairmen specifically took note of the "hazards of retrospective judgement". However a subsequent report by a Select Committee of the Legislative Council was much more critical of some officials. In mid-2004, following its publication, the Secretary for Health, Welfare and Food (i.e. the Minister) Dr E K Yeoh, resigned to accept responsibility.

Some of the treatments adopted were found to have long term adverse effects on the health of "recovered" patients. Whatever the fumbling of officials, no one in the community doubted that the front line medical personnel had saved Hong Kong with their courage, dedication and sheer professionalism.

IT IS DIFFICULT, writing even just six years after SARS, to capture the full flavour of the panic that struck the community at the time and the direct and immediate economic impact.

One minute the most bustling city in the world was pursuing business opportunities around the globe with its customary fervour, the next the whole place was virtually shut down.

The airline and tourism industries were devastated: no-one wanted to visit Hong Kong – the city of masks. James Hughes-Hallett, then local head of Swire Pacific, the conglomerate that owns the local airline Cathay Pacific, was to say in a speech to a business meeting some months later that he could confirm some planes had been flying with the number of passengers in single digits, adding dryly "and could I remind some of you that nought is a single digit". The planes had to be in the air because of the contracts to move cargo – the aircraft holds were bursting with the goods from southern China that had become an integral part of global supply chains. But unless there were really compelling circumstances, people didn't have to move.

Hotel occupancy plummeted. One night, the world-famous Peninsula Hotel had just three paying guests. By chance I was having lunch the next day with a director of the company who asked "Would you like a room? Hell, would you like a floor?" There were reports that even the Mandarin Hotel was offering room-rates of a mere $600 per night[1] (a fraction of the normal rate) just to try to get some people through the door.

Restaurants were similarly devastated. At the height of the panic it was possible to enter the most popular restaurants at 1 pm without a lunch reservation, and command a table by the window. While there was a certain pleasure in being made welcome where one might previously have only been tolerated, no-one could enjoy the fact that the consequences for the overall economy must surely be awful.

And they were. Official statistics back up the anecdotal evidence quoted above. Hotel occupancy that in normal times motored steadily along in the 80-90% range suddenly plummeted to 20% or less. GDP figures that had begun a quiet recovery starting from mid-2002 (Q3: +2.8%; Q4: +4.8%; 2003: Q1 +4.1% – all year-on-year in constant prices) suddenly slipped into reverse (2003 Q2: –0.9%). There were immediate consequences for unemployment: the rate had levelled off in mid-2002 at about 7.5% as Hong Kong's economy adjusted to the after-effects of the Asian economic meltdown of the late 1990s and the subsequent bursting of the property price bubble. Suddenly in the spring of 2003 the rate began to shoot up (2/2003 - 4/2003: 7.8%; 3/2003 - 5/2003: 8.2%; 4/2003 - 6/2003: 8.5%).

And just as foreigners were steering clear of Hong Kong, so other places did not welcome our visits. On a routine investment promotion mission to Tokyo in June, we booked our usual hotel. Somewhat to our surprise my colleague and I were told it would not be necessary to check in at the front desk. Because we were such good customers we would be met at the front door and allowed to complete check-in formalities in our rooms. At first flattered at the special treatment, we later discovered the real reason. The hotel had concluded it could not refuse the booking because it obtained so much business from the Hong Kong Government but at the same time did not want people at the front desk announcing in front of other guests that they were from Hong Kong. Needless to say by the time of my next visit, when SARS was well past, the special front door greeting disappeared.

Government Response

THE GOVERNMENT KNEW it would have to act quickly and de-cisively if it was to head off widespread social discontent, which was already stirring because of the various issues discussed earlier which formed the political backdrop. Hence the response to the economic impact of SARS was striking in its scale and fairly comprehensive in its coverage. On 23 April 2003, the Chief Executive Tung Chee Hwa announced a package of measures costing a total $11.8 billion of which $11.7 billion would be borne by the Government, the bal-ance by the Housing Authority (HA).

The package comprised $5.4 billion in loss of revenue ($5.3 billion by the Government, $100 million by HA) and $6.4 billion in additional expenditure.

The revenue foregone included Rates Concessions ($2.6 bil-lion), Water, Sewage and Trade Effluent Surcharge Concessions ($521 million), Licensing Fees Concessions ($276 million), Salaries Tax Rebate ($2.3 billion), Housing Authority Commercial Rent Concessions ($205 million, shared equally by the Government and the HA) and Government Rent Concessions ($72 million).

The additional expenditure covered Creation of New Jobs and Training Places ($282 million) Creation of 3000 temporary street cleaning jobs in the Food and Environmental Hygiene Department for six months for cleaning up Hong Kong ($150 million) Relief Loan Guarantee and Associated Cost ($3.5 billion) Provisional Sum for Disease Control ($1.5 billion) and Provisional Sum for Measures to Revive Economy ($1 billion).

As can be seen, the idea was to give something to everyone because the whole community was feeling the strain, but at the same time to concentrate the relief measures on those hardest hit. For example the salaries tax rebate was set at 50% of the final 2001 -2 demand, but capped at $3,000. The new and temporary jobs focused on those at the lower end of the employment spectrum, most of the rates and fee concessions targeted Small and Medium sized Enterprises.

The main purpose of announcing such a big package was to show that the Government was serious about dealing with SARS in the short, medium and long term. There was money to nail the outbreak, money to help the community get through a difficult spell, and a large provisional sum to help relaunch the economy when the storm had passed.

On 10 April, the then Financial Secretary Antony Leung spoke to me in the margins of a meeting on a different subject (the proposal to further develop Ocean Park). He said he had spoken to my then boss, then Secretary for Commerce, Industry and Technology (SCIT) Henry Tang, and asked if he could borrow my services on a part-time basis to handle the work relating to the economic relaunch effort that would become necessary once SARS had been contained. He said an unconventional approach would be required if it were to be successful and he had heard I had a reputation for "out of the box" thinking. Tang had agreed to my undertaking these additional duties, but it was the common understanding that my primary duties as head of InvestHK were not to be sacrificed and should continue as normal. The relaunch work was to be squeezed in as a part-time extra assignment. Subsequently I worked closely with Leung and other officials on economic relaunch while maintaining my role as head of the investment promotion agency. Within the department, I selected one deputy (Ophelia Tsang) and one team head (David Chiu) to assist me on a part-time basis in addition to their existing duties. Other general support work would also inevitably fall on our small administrative team which was now seriously stretched.

The Financial Secretary formed two bodies to help him steer

the Economic Relaunch programme. The first, called the Economic Relaunch Working Group (ERWG), was comprised of five Ministers, one other political appointee and two civil servants. The five were Leung himself who would chair, the Secretary for Home Affairs Patrick Ho, the Secretary for Economic Development and Labour Stephen Ip, the Secretary for Financial Services and the Treasury Fred Ma, and Tang; the political appointee was the Director of the Chief Executive's Office W K Lam; the two civil servants were the Director of Information Services Yvonne Choi, and myself as secretary. For administrative convenience, it was decided that the funds for relaunch would be placed under the departmental vote for InvestHK which I am responsible for administering. However, ERWG would make all the decisions on which projects to support and decide how much should be spent. Therefore in respect of the $105 million p.a. for investment promotion I was the "Controlling Officer" in both name and substance because I had discretion how to spend the money, but for the $1 billion relaunch fund I was controller in name only, my job being simply to dispense the sums as determined by ERWG.

The second body was called the Economic Relaunch Strategy Group (ERSG), and it comprised the members of ERWG plus a number of members of the community including representatives of the tourism industry and the commercial sector. They were: dean of the School of Business & Management at the Hong Kong University of Science and Technology K C Chan; president of the Chinese Manufacturers' Association Chan Wing Kee; chairman of the Hong Kong Tourism Board Selina Chow; lecturer at City University Ivan Choy; chairman of the Hong Kong Airport Authority Victor Fung; president of the Hong Kong Japanese Chamber of Commerce & Industry Ryota Honjo; chairman of the Federation of Hong Kong Industries Victor Lo; chairman of the British Chamber of Commerce Norman Lyle; chairman of the HK General Chamber of Commerce Anthony Nightingale; chairman of the HK Association of Banks Raymond Or; chairman of the American Chamber of Commerce

Jim Thompson; vice-chairman of the Chinese General Chamber of Commerce Philip Wong; executive director of the HK Federation of Youth Groups Rosanna Wong; chairman of the HK Policy Research Institute Paul Yip; chairman of the HK Retail Management Association P C Yu; chief executive of the Better Hong Kong Foundation George Yuen and vice chairman of the HK Chinese Enterprises Association Zhou Jie.

ERSG was to give an overall steer on the programme and help secure community buy-in for the work. Inevitably, InvestHK morphed into becoming the supporting agency of the Economic Relaunch programme, including providing the secretariat for both ERWG and ERSG. We devised the procedures for inviting relaunch ideas, processing them, and distributing the funds in accordance with ERWG's decisions. All this produced an enormous volume of work, all without provision of additional staff resources.

The $1 billion set aside for this purpose had interesting provenance: it was simply a figure plucked from the air for the purpose of sounding big and determined. When InvestHK was effectively given responsibility for administering what became known as the Economic Relaunch programme, one of the first things we had to do was prepare a submission to the Finance Committee of the Legislative Council to justify the expenditure. No-one could tell us where the $1 billion figure had come from. Moreover a call circular to all corners of the Administration seeking suggestions for economic relaunch produced ideas which would cost only a little over $700 million. Most of that – some $400 million – was related to tourism. In order to reach the magic prescribed total we added in $200 million for what were termed "Mega Events", added a healthy dollop of contingency, and there we were: $1 billion as instructed. The Ministers endorsed this approach.

ERWG decided at an early meeting that there would be three levels of government involvement in projects: those where the government acted as the organiser, those where it acted as co-organiser, and those where it acted merely as sponsor. The degree of government involvement in the actual running of an event would be set accordingly. This was not simply a matter of semantics. When an organisation (in this case, the Government) takes on the role of organiser or co-organiser, it has or shares responsibility for how the event is run and how money is expended. But in the case of sponsorship, the relationship is different. The organiser is responsible for running the event including handling the budget. He offers a package of benefits and quotes a sponsorship fee. The potential sponsor decides whether the benefits are commensurate with the fee quoted and on this basis decides whether or not to go ahead and enter into a contract to buy those benefits. In these cases, the money is "spent" by the sponsor when it is handed over to the organiser.

InvestHK had, and has, a great deal of experience in considering sponsorship proposals. In its early years the department sponsored the Fortune Global Forum (2001), the Forbes Global CEO Conference (2002), the Business Week CEO Conference (2003) among other events, all with the view of raising the city's profile as the best place in Asia for business. These are only some high-profile examples. The department receives scores of sponsorship proposals annually, evaluates them as marketing tools, and sponsors those it considers provide value for money. In no instance does the department organise, or co-organise, a sponsored event.

ERWG also agreed that the different Ministers ("policy secretaries" in Hong Kong parlance) would have responsibility for the activities which fell within their policy remit. Policy Bureaus, or departments with their support, would bring forward individual proposals for ERWG consideration. Even where the genesis of an idea had come from the wider community, it still needed a backer within the government to support and take ownership of it. Altogether ERWG considered 95 different relaunch ideas and decided to support 84 of them. Of these, 83 had a clearly defined Minister.

There was to be only *one* exception. Because of the way the proposal was generated and considered, the suggestion by the American Chamber of Commerce in Hong Kong (AmCham) that it organise an international entertainment festival with govern-ment support did not have a departmental backer at the outset, and hence the project later known as HarbourFest *did not have a Minister with assigned responsibility and accountability.*

Sidebar:
The Establishment of InvestHK

IN ORDER TO understand how an investment promotion agency came to have responsibility for a pop music festival, it is necessary to review how the agency came about.

Prior to 2000, Hong Kong had never had a dedicated investment promotion agency. A small team in the Industry Department – called the "One Stop Unit" – had the task of assisting potential investors in the manufacturing sector, but given that Hong Kong's own manufacturers were busy decamping to the Pearl River Delta as China opened up its economy to the outside world, this was very much an uphill battle. It became clear that Hong Kong was fast transforming itself into a services economy and that a new stand-alone department was needed to target companies in specific sectors where Hong Kong had a competitive edge and/or which added more economic value.

In his budget speech in March 2000, the FS (still at that time Tsang) announced that a new department would be established from 1 July 2000. The department would be called Invest Hong Kong – which quickly transmogrified to InvestHK – and I was asked to be the first head of it, with the title Director-General of Investment Promotion (DGIP). Naturally this was a great honour, but also slightly intimidating.

By early 2001 we had identified the nine economic sectors to which we would give priority and structured the head office so that we had nine sector teams which would each seek to attract companies from their target sector irrespective of where in the world the company was headquartered.

In order to get the Hong Kong product better known out in the market, we also embarked on a demanding schedule of overseas investment promotion missions. Many of these I led myself, especially in the early days. But even when I eased off slightly, I was still spending close to one quarter of my working time overseas. A typical year would include eight week-long long-haul missions (two to North America, two to Europe, one to Japan/Korea, one to Australasia, one to India and the Gulf, and one to a second-tier target market – usually in latter years to South America). This would be supplemented by short (one or two day) trips to Singapore and Taiwan (maybe once per year each) and Mainland China where I tried to go on average once per month in an effort to overcome past neglect. (By the time I left the department in 2008, Mainland companies were close to 20% of our live project caseload.)

A typical trip would cover one key city per day. For example, on my very last mission to North America, the programme covered Toronto, Washington, Minneapolis, San Diego and Los Angeles, a Sunday-to-Sunday programme including two days of trans-Pacific travel, and back in the office on Monday morning. (It doesn't get much better than that!)

Our initial budget was set at $65 million p.a. (much less than initially recommended, and only a fraction of what Singapore spends on similar activities) and we had about 70 staff in the Hong Kong headquarters. In early 2003 it was decided that our investment promotion work should be given a short-term boost and we were allocated an additional sum of $200 million to be spread over five years. Thus our annual budget grew to about $105 million, i.e. an increase of about two-thirds for our core investment promotion duties. All of the time-limited extra resources would be devoted to hiring extra front line staff within Hong Kong itself and additional representation in overseas markets. There was no corresponding increase in support personnel and the additional workload was to be simply absorbed.

There is one further InvestHK duty I should mention. For various historical reasons, I had retained personal responsibility for taking forward the project to build a new exhibition centre in Hong Kong. AsiaWorld-Expo as it became known was to open ahead of schedule and within budget at the end of 2005. The reason for including a reference to it here is that the worldwide tender exercise reached its climax in the summer of 2003 – as if we didn't have enough on our plate!

Birth of the Idea

HARBOURFEST, therefore, was born out of the perceived urgent need to rejuvenate Hong Kong's economy and self-confidence.

The vast majority of ideas for economic relaunch came from within the Government. However it was realised from the outset that it was important to involve the whole community in the re-launch programme. With this spirit in mind, Leung used his position as chairman of ERSG to appeal for ideas from the community, at its first and second meetings (10 and 23 May respectively). Indeed, after the second meeting he led the whole group to meet the media.

Then AmCham chairman Jim Thompson, being a member of ERSG and head of the largest international chamber, took his responsibilities seriously and took the initiative to circulate to all members of the chamber an appeal for suggestions. The Sports and Entertainment Committee (chairman Mike Denzel of the NBA, vice chairman Jon Niermann of Disney) came up with the idea of an international entertainment festival which they would organise with the help of other AmCham members with experience in the entertainment field. The thinking was very provisional at first, more in the way of a concept than a firm proposal, and included things like a basketball tournament as well as concerts. The idea was that there would be something for all the family, there would be events to attract locals and the resident expatriate population, as well as draw in visitors from around the region. Ticket prices were to be nominal only since the whole purpose was to get people out of their houses to resume normal life, and show the world that Hong Kong was alive and kicking. The thinking was that they would not be lured by a run of the mill entertainment event at standard commercial rates. There needed to be some big name stars with tickets at giveaway prices. The AmCham team approached InvestHK, being the government's contact point for relaunch suggestions, to discuss the idea on 5 June.

Given the scale of the proposal (right from the outset AmCham took as a reference the $200 million earmarked for mega events, and requested a government subsidy of $100 million) it was clearly necessary to get views from other departments and in particular from the Leisure and Cultural Services Department (LCSD) which managed government-owned entertainment venues and also organised similar events. An inter-departmental meeting was pulled together by InvestHK on 26 June to take a preliminary look at AmCham's proposal. Representatives of the Tourism Commission, LCSD and the Environmental Protection Department attended. The Home Affairs Bureau, which had policy responsibility for entertainment, had also been invited but its representative was absent with apologies. This seemed a small point at the time, but it was to have major implications later. The conclusion of the meeting was that the idea seemed to fit the criteria the government had announced, and was bold enough to capture attention and "jerk" the community back to normalcy. However given the amount of money involved in both absolute and relative terms – the proposed government subsidy of $100 million made up the lion's share of a total budget of $116 million – it could not be handled at working level. AmCham should make a presentation of their proposal direct to ERWG.

At this stage, there was no clearly identified Minister to take ownership of the proposal as there was no department proposing support for it. It was simply AmCham's idea, which an inter-departmental meeting thought was worthy of ERWG's consideration.

Decision Making Process

ALTHOUGH THE DECISION to support the event which became known as HarbourFest was in a sense a single one, it is probably more helpful to think of it as a package of decisions made up of different elements. Some of those elements were, with the benefit of hindsight, simply wrong. Some, while possibly sensible in themselves, nonetheless clashed with other elements.

Amcham's proposal was scrutinised twice by the ERWG, on 2 and 12 July.

On the first occasion, the idea was endorsed in principle subject to our department (somehow, we had become the subject department responsible) being satisfied with the budget. I was told later by those attending that the total time spent by the meeting considering the idea was about 30 minutes, the bulk of which – some 20-25 minutes – was taken up by AmCham's presentation. There had apparently been relatively little discussion. Later, when the subject had become controversial, the official memory was revised and the party line changed to 45 minutes.

At the second meeting, ERWG confirmed its previous decision to support the event with a subsidy of up to $100 million as requested by AmCham. Again, there was reportedly relatively little discussion, though a last minute condition was included to require ticket prices to be set close to normal commercial levels. But there was no change to the basic relationship of the parties. The terms of the decision were quite explicit as recorded in the minutes of the meeting:

He [i.e. Leung] also emphasised that the Government would act

24

as the sponsor only. AmCham had to plan, organise and implement the whole event.

I had not been able to attend either of these ERWG meetings
because they clashed with important long-standing work commit-
ments critical to the performance of my mainstream DGIP duties.
The week of 2 July, I had been in North America conducting an investment promotion mission and indeed on the day itself was making a speech to a business group. The meeting on 12 July coincided
with the final negotiating session on the AsiaWorld-Expo project.
However I was represented at both sessions by Ophelia Tsang and
David Chiu, and briefed by them afterwards on necessary follow-up
action.

At no time, then or later, did ERWG or anyone else make a
determination as to which Minister should have political responsibility for HarbourFest. On the one hand, since it was an entertainment event directed at raising public morale, it should fall under
the policy area of Patrick Ho in Home Affairs. That would argue for
one of his departments – the Leisure and Cultural Services Department was the obvious one – being the executive agency. A possible
alternative, since one objective was to help revive tourism, was for
Stephen Ip to be responsible with the Tourism Commission acting as his executive arm. In the event, InvestHK was identified as
the sponsoring department but without it being formally confirmed
that Tang was the Minister responsible.

Thus were sown the seeds for confusion. Shortly afterwards
there was a change of personnel at the Minister level, Tang moving
up to FS after Leung's resignation (he resigned on 16 July, Tang became FS in early August), and John Tsang moving from the post of
Permanent Secretary for Housing & Development to become SCIT.
Henry Tang had never taken ownership of HarbourFest as SCIT,
and John Tsang declined to do so for essentially the same reasons
(i.e. "It is an entertainment event, which falls way outside my area
of expertise and policy responsibility").

THE POTENTIAL DIFFICULTIES in the proposal were clear at the time. These were:

(a) *Lead Time*. Most people in the entertainment industry who made their views known felt a lead time of 12-15 months was needed to mount a successful festival on the scale proposed. On the other hand, if the event was to contribute to the relaunch of the Hong Kong economy, it needed to be held as soon as possible. AmCham undertook to hold the first concert within 100 days and complete the whole series within one month.

(b) *Scale of the event*. Given the relatively short lead time, and bearing in mind the scale of the event, it was for consideration whether it was practicable to stage 17 concerts spread over four weeks or whether it would have been better to be more modest and go with two or three concerts held during a single (long) weekend.

(c) *Financial Commitment*. Directly related to (b), it was for consideration whether the Government should have agreed a sponsorship fee of up to $100 million, or whether it would have been better to go with a smaller sum, say $20-25 million. The AmCham proposal was purposely ambitious in keeping with the spirit of the Financial Secretary's call for urgent action. ERWG endorsed the plan.

(d) *Venue*. ERWG accepted the budget which provided for importation and erection of a special stage on the reclamation next to Tamar naval base. The option of using an existing venue such as the Government Stadium, which would have been much cheaper, was not considered.

(e) *Format*. ERWG and ERSG were comfortable with AmCham's idea of a local artist and an imported one being together on the same bill. This proved controversial as the artists tended to attract different audiences, one would inevitably be seen as junior to the other and there was a suggestion that the local artists should work for nominal fees only as it was their community that was being rescued, whereas for the overseas talent this was just a job. This potential complication was not identified by any party during the project consideration stage.

(f) *Degree of Government Involvement.* ERWG endorsed the AmCham proposal that the government should be a sponsor only and that AmCham should have sole responsibility for planning, organising and implementing the whole event. Given the very short lead time compared to the scale of the event, a simplified management structure was essential. On the other hand, given the amount of public money involved, there was a community expectation (later manifested) that the government would keep a tight hold on the purse strings more commensurate with an organiser or at least co-organiser role. This potential political hiccup was not identified at the outset.

(g) *Subject Department.* At its 2 July meeting, ERWG had identified InvestHK as the subject department to be responsible for scrutinising the budget. The role of InvestHK as sponsoring agent was confirmed at the 12 July meeting. As long as the role was purely one of sponsor, InvestHK was qualified to do the job. However, if it had been the intention that the government should have a more hands-on role such as organiser or co-organiser, then the Leisure and Cultural Services Department (LCSD) would have been a more appropriate agency. LCSD after all had some experience in organising entertainment events whereas InvestHK had none.

(h) *Ticket Pricing Strategy.* AmCham's original proposal was that ticket prices should be set at nominal levels only in order to fill the venue on every occasion and to drive home the message that life in Hong Kong had returned to its usual vibrant self. However, at the last minute at the 12 July meeting ERWG imposed a condition that ticket prices should be set at normal commercial levels. This was with the apparent aim of reducing the amount of sponsorship fee if possible below the agreed ceiling of $100 million. Such a radical change in the ethos of the event was to have a major effect on the outcome. For one thing, it resulted in the concerts to some extent competing with each other ("Should we go to see Prince or save the money for the Rolling Stones") which in turn meant some concerts did not attract a full house and therefore earned less revenue. This side-effect of what was a no doubt well-intended change was overlooked when the decision was made, and was not challenged at the time by AmCham.

BE ALL THIS AS IT MAY, InvestHK and AmCham then got down to business. Because of the very short time available before the first concert, several things that would normally have happened sequentially had to be tackled in parallel. For example, it would be usual to set everything out in a formal contract document before implementing arrangements and incurring expenditure. In the case of HarbourFest, drafting of the sponsorship agreement was put in hand immediately but work on preparing the site and lining up artists to appear could not wait for the lawyers. AmCham's legal team produced one draft of a possible agreement and InvestHK produced a radically different one. The InvestHK version took as a model a previous sponsorship deal which had been approved from a legal perspective by the Department of Justice and which had served its purposes well. (It had been used for sponsoring the Forbes Global CEO Conference in 2002). In consultation with the Department of Justice (with whom we communicated by telephone call and email throughout the process, and also brought in to key meetings) we then reconciled the two versions which naturally took time. In the event, final agreement on the contract was not reached until early October, a week before the first concert.

Sponsorship agreements often provide for payment of the fee in stages as arrangements proceed and the event itself gets closer. In the case of HarbourFest, staged payments had to be made before the contract was finally settled because not to have done so would have derailed the whole event. AmCham could not have entered into artist and other contracts without the cash to cover outgoings, and revenue from ticket sales and commercial sponsorship would only come in later. The interim payments – there were three, each of

$25 million -- were documented by simple legal documents (called "Memoranda of Understanding", or "MoUs") which were swept up in the final contract at which point the final instalment, also of $25 million, was handed over. The contract contained a provision that if for any reason the shortfall on HarbourFest was less than $100 million, the balance had to be returned to the Government. This arrangement thereby met the ERWG decision that the sponsorship was to "up to" $100 million.

HarbourFest: The Event

IT IS NOT EASY to characterise the HarbourFest event in a single word or phrase. From a narrow logistic perspective, the staging of the event was a miracle; the quality of many of the concerts was outstanding; ticket sales for some of them were disappointing; politically, it was a nightmare.

The "miracle" started with the site itself: it was operating as a public carpark at the time HarbourFest got the go-ahead. The operator's lease was due to expire on 30 September. He was told straight away in mid-July it would not be extended and although this possibility had been included in the tenancy document, he did not raise objections, did not try to linger and moved off smoothly by midnight of the magic day. Various contractors working on or near the site were informed of the planned use and all managed to complete their work, or re-schedule it, so as not to interfere. The stage was imported by container from Australia. The ship arrived on schedule, the whole venue was erected within the first two weeks of October, the sound system turned out to be fabulous once installed, and the Environmental Protection Department conducted tests which showed noise levels did not exceed the statutory limits even when the amplifiers were at normal pop concert levels. (And it didn't rain for a single one of the seventeen concerts. Even God was doing His part.)

Finalising the artist line-up was like herding cats. Whenever AmCham's agent thought he had an act firmed up so that other pieces of the jigsaw could be fit in round it, something would go wrong. Cher agreed to appear as part of her farewell world tour; the fee was US$1 million, and in accordance with industry practice a

50% deposit was paid up front. Great! – a world name to kick off the event. Then the lady changed her mind, saying she was too tired. Even though the deposit was reimbursed in full without difficulty, this was a real loss.

Jay Chou, a popular Taiwan singer, also signed up but backed out. He had been interested in performing because he was crazy about basketball and the early plans included an appearance by some top NBA names. But when the police reversed an earlier agreement to close adjacent roads (necessary for the basketball element to go ahead), the NBA idea had to be cancelled and Jay lost interest.

Atomic Kitten, a girl group, signed up to do a show on the same bill with Tatu (two reputed lesbian singers who would kiss with open mouth on stage) and Twins, a popular local female duo with a somewhat more sedate image (at least at that time). At the last minute, one of the Kittens fell sick. Although their fee was fully reimbursed, the other two groups had been contracted to appear so the show had to go on. But without the lead act, how could tickets sell at the originally set price? And there remained the issue of how to handle refunds to those who had already purchased tickets. In the event, the problem was "solved" by making all tickets free. There would be a 100% refund for those who had bought tickets. They would be allowed to keep the tickets as well! There would be free distribution of the remainder on a first-come-first-served basis. Incredibly there would still be criticism of this arrangement because some people who queued for free tickets failed to get one.

Prince had been out of the pop limelight for several years because of a dispute with his record company (for a while he was known as "the artist formerly known as Prince", apparently because the other party owned the IP rights to the name) but agreed to perform on the opening night as his comeback concert. The trouble was he was dealing with all contractual matters himself, not always efficiently. Faxes to his home went unanswered for days or weeks when only hours were available. This created huge problems when trying to line up the local star to appear with him. Anita Mui, probably the most popular female singer of the time, had agreed to open the show with Prince. Subsequently she added a proviso – she would only do so if he would agree to dance with her on stage. So a desperate fax was sent to the USA where it was ignored for several days. By the time Prince had recovered from his surprise at the unusual request and had agreed, Mui had decided she wanted to compere rather than sing (a change possibly brought about by health problems; while it was known that she had been unwell, it was not realised that the illness was terminal). At this point Am-Cham pulled the plug and brought in another local star Karen Mok to take Mui's place. Finally the tickets for the first concert could go on sale.

So far, pretty much par for the course for those familiar with the entertainment industry. But it was the on again/off again saga with the Rolling Stones – much of it played out in the full glare of the media spotlight – that really proved to be a show in its own right.

The idea of bring the Rolling Stones to Hong Kong had first been put forward by an independent promoter, Colleen Ironside. The Government, represented by the Home Affairs Bureau, was supportive. However, before the plans could be firmed up, the Har-bourFest proposal had come forward and had been speedily en-dorsed. It didn't make sense for the Government to be supporting two different highly subsidised entertainment events, so the obvious thing to do was put the parties in touch. This we did and AmCham and Ironside got down to negotiations. At one point it seemed as though a deal had been done (InvestHK was not involved in the detailed negotiations – after all we were a sponsor only – but we tried to keep in touch with progress as part of our support role). Ironside would get free use of the Tamar venue for the night, col-lect all revenue from ticket sales, and get a cash subsidy from the AmCham event budget. Just when it seemed that everything was smooth sailing, the talks broke down. Exactly why, and who should bear responsibility, are matters beyond my ken. But the result was that AmCham began to deal direct with Stones management, who of course were aware that time was running out, while an embittered Ironside sat on the sidelines. Eventually an agreement was reached on dates, fee, and special arrangements (separate insurance for Mick's throat, a pool table for Keith, etc).

The draft contract and half the fee were forwarded on 2 October, but the Stones management team refused to sign or allow tickets to go on sale. The main stumbling block seemed to be the desire to include concerts in Beijing and Shanghai as part of the Asian itinerary. The Stones management were unable to sort this out for themselves, and then tried to make approval of these concerts the responsibility of AmCham in Hong Kong. Frenzied discussions took place and at AmCham's request InvestHK became directly involved in order to impress on the Stones' management the seriousness of the situation. Because of location of the band members themselves and their various lawyers, the telephone calls always seemed to take place after midnight HK time.

Eventually AmCham drew a line in the sand and set a deadline of midnight 9 October for signature of the contract. This was necessary in order to allow sufficient time to market the tickets before the scheduled dates for the concerts (7 & 9 November). When Thompson announced publicly on 10 October that the Stones would not be appearing, the Stones management finally grasped that Hong Kong was serious and told Reuters news agency that the show would after all go on. They then signed the contract and on 15 October, Thompson and I were obliged to conduct a joint press conference to try to explain why the concerts would, after all, go ahead.

The media had a field day with all this. Some of the early headlines in the South China Morning Post were fairly neutral in tone – "Stones offered $5 million to play Tamar" (31 August); "Stones, Jay Chou and Santana sign up for Tamar show" (4 September) – but the stories themselves could contain wild inaccuracies, including a false allegation of overpayment of artist fee.

But it did not take long for critics to come out of the wood-work, including of course some with a vested interest (never disclosed or mentioned in the article)[1]: "Critics question $80 million festival pledge" (5 September); "Gala sounds note of discord" (8 September), "Fest seeking local stars for free; While overseas performers are being offered millions, HK acts are urged to do their patriotic duty" (11 September); "Music fest organisers refuse to detail cost; Taxpayers subsidising post-SARS bash won't be told how their money is spent" and "Public money requires a public accounting" (both 12 September); "Fest bosses snubbed experts free help" (13 September).

The generally negative coverage continued into October "Stones pullout draws criticism" (12 October); "Rowse refuses to respond to music fest critics" (22 October). At least this last story was true: I refused to allow a routine press conference on investment promotion (which was, after all, my full time job) to be hijacked by HarbourFest.

Some of the other stories were simply false or built around single source fabrications, but some of the negative stories were justified. Ticket sales to some of the early shows were disappointing. Both Prince and Craig David on the first two nights fell a long way short of selling out and naturally the focus was on empty seats. The crowd for José Carreras of something over 5,000 was his biggest audience for years[2], but the venue could have held 12,500.

A particular weakness of the AmCham organisation, and InvestHK's support, was the absence of a compelling Cantonese-speaking spokesperson to handle the media. The expression "feed the beast, or the beast will eat you" was never more true than at this time. It could have been pointed out, for example, that the venue had been sized to cope with the most popular artists and it was inevitable that some shows would not fill it given that tickets were now at commercial rates. This is such an obvious common sense point, but there was no-one to put it across in Chinese, so it was ignored by the Chinese-language media.

And as fast as the bad press gathered speed, so the politicians jumped on the bandwagon and the Ministers ran away. The problem began as early as the launch press conference scheduled for 3 September. In the days leading up to it, we tried to get a government Minister to attend together with AmCham. As this was an entertainment event, the obvious candidate was Secretary for Home Affairs Patrick Ho. However, a phone call to his office, in which we explained why we were calling, was not returned. In the event, I took part in the press conference myself (as part of the support role we had promised ERSG that we would play).

FS Henry Tang signed an open letter on 25 September confirming the Government's full support for the Festival and its role as the major sponsor with a view to facilitating AmCham in the procurement of commercial sponsorship. However, two specific letters addressed to named potential major sponsors (around $4 million each) which had been sent to his office for signature at the same time were never returned. One company chose to go ahead with its sponsorship anyway, but the other – a large American financial institution – withdrew. Similarly, Tang declined to issue a general e-mail urging civil servants to attend, though one was later issued by Chief Secretary Donald Tsang.

The Financial Affairs Panel of LegCo arranged a special meeting on 25 September to discuss HarbourFest. When I pointed out I would be out of town on a duty trip elsewhere the meeting was postponed to 3 October. One by one all the ministerial members of ERWG made their excuses about why they could not attend, until only two civil servants – Yvonne Choi and myself – had agreed to go. Even the Ministers could see that this would create a scandal, so Tang procured a further delay, to 11 October, and ordered all Ministers to be there with him.

Apart from this unwillingness to be too closely associated with HarbourFest, other ministerial decisions dealt a more direct financial blow to the event. It was decided for the purposes of the tenancy agreement between the Lands Department and AmCham for use of the site that the latter would be treated as a normal commercial tenant – notwithstanding the fact that the event was part of the Government's own Economic Relaunch programme – and charged rent, $1 million per month for October and November. Tang declined to intervene in the negotiations so an already stretched budget had to find another $2 million. (Part of the deposit, which also had to be paid, was not refunded at the conclusion of the event in order to cover the cost of removing some blue paint used to mark out the site. This became another unbudgeted expense though as the site was scheduled to be used for development it was not clear why the paint had to be removed, or indeed if it ever was.) When HarbourFest was first launched, a TV advertisement was prepared and broadcast using part of the Government's free air time known as APIs or Announcements of Public Interest. However the TV stations claimed this was a misuse of the facility (economic relaunch was not in the public interest?) so the free broadcasts were ordered to cease. The marketing value thus lost had to be replaced by expensive paid advertising, and by distribution of free tickets.

Those of us at the sharp end never resolved which individual or body was responsible for making all these decisions which were having such a negative impact on HarbourFest. The decision to charge full commercial ticket prices was made by the full ERWG, apparently after behind the scene lobbying by the entertainment industry. It was a mistake, but at least it was made in the open. Who decided to scrap the use of the APIs? Or to charge rent for use of the site? (To avoid criticism? By whom?) Or not to sign the letters to individual sponsors? At the meetings where these decisions were made, who was making the case to *support* HarbourFest? Certainly not anyone from InvestHK, as we were not invited.

From being heroes out to help save Hong Kong, the AmCham volunteers – and, by association, the part-time InvestHK support team – were now being cast as villains. And the Ministers who had made the original decision, well intended though it was, were too busy trying to be invisible to defend it or those implementing it.

BUT DESPITE ALL the problems – and the above is by no means a complete list – the final HarbourFest programme was impressive:

October

    17 Prince; Karen Mok

    18 (am) Family Fest (a variety show for children)

    18 Craig David

    19 (am) Family Fest

    20 Jose Carreras; Charlotte Church

    24 Tatu; Twins

    25 Westlife; Energy; Yvonne Hsu

    26 Air Supply; Ronald Cheng; Eason Chan

    29 Umoja charity premier (held in Lyric Theatre)

    30 Gypsy Kings with Danny Diaz

    31 Asian All Stars

November

    1 Santana; Andy Hui

    2 Gary Valenciano (popular Filipino artist) 2 shows

    6 Neil Young; Michelle Branch

    7 Rolling Stones; Mick Gerace

    8 Rolling Stones; Nicholas Tse; Joey Yung

The Director of Audit Report

THERE WERE altogether three official inquiries into what became popularly, albeit perhaps unfairly, known as the "HarbourFest Fiasco". The first was by the Director of Audit, the second by a so-called "Independent" Panel of Inquiry, and the third by the Public Accounts Committee (PAC) of the Legislative Council. Nominally, this last is a normal follow-up to the audit report though in this case publication was held back to also take on board the main findings of the "Independent" Panel.

The Director of Audit is formally appointed by the Chief Executive, normally on the recommendation of the Financial Secretary. The appointment of Benjamin Tang Kwok Bun as Director of Audit in December 2003 had been controversial. "Tung pressed to replace audit director" ran one headline in the SCMP on 29 November. "A LegCo committee says Benjamin Tang has the wrong background for the job." The story generated a fair bit of steam in the following days as follow-up SCMP headlines showed. "I'll show you, says embattled auditor" (30 November); "New auditor shrugs off controversy to start work" (2 December); and even "Tung admits audit chief not first choice" (5 December).

The then chairman of the PAC was the elected representative of the Accountants Functional Constituency Eric Li Ka Cheung. Li objected strongly to the appointment on the grounds that Tang was not qualified for the job as he had no accountancy background. (Nor for that matter did he have any experience in the Finance Branch of the Government, which might have partially offset the lack of formal qualifications.) "Since many administrative officers are in positions of power, Mr Tang's relationship with them may, in reality or in the public's perception, affect his judgement and decision." Li was quoted as saying.

IT WAS INEVITABLE that HarbourFest would be the subject of an audit investigation. The key question for me was whether the Director would accept that the project was an AmCham initiative which the Government had chosen to sponsor, or treat it as a Government project which the Government had selected AmCham to run.

In the event auditor Tang chose both alternatives at the same time.

The report, published in March 2004, was like the proverbial parson's egg: good in parts. In paragraph 6.10 of the report, in the section on lessons to be learned, the Director got to the root of the problem:

> sponsorship may not be a suitable arrangement to finance a project which is largely funded by the Government

That, in a nutshell, was the issue. As he himself had pointed out earlier in his report (para 2.28), the original budget submitted by AmCham envisaged a Government contribution of $100 million out of a total budget of $116 million, i.e. the Government was providing 86% of the total. Even after a substantial increase in both revenue and costs, with the Government sponsorship fee remaining the same, the Government's share was 64%. As the Director went on to say in paragraph 2.34,

> Given that the Government paid for the bulk of the cost of HarbourFest, and in view of the need to account for such a large sum of public expenditure, Audit considers that sponsorship did not seem to be an appropriate form of financing this project.

Exactly so.

But having got the analysis almost perfectly correct, the report went on to muddy the water. The same paragraph goes on to say:

> Audit has not seen documentary evidence indicating that, before the decision to finance the Harbour Fest by way of sponsorship was made, the pros and cons of doing so, vis-a-vis other options of financing (e.g. by way of other forms of government grants) had been thoroughly examined and submitted to the ERWG for consideration.

The key to the Audit oversight is use of the passive voice: it cleverly masks the fact that no-one is identified as being responsible for this failure. At the point of first submission of the proposal on 2 July, there was no government department responsible for HarbourFest, it was simply an AmCham proposal which that organisation was putting to the Government for consideration. InvestHK, in its limited capacity as part-time secretariat for ERWG, ERSG and relaunch generally, had received the proposal, ensured it had received preliminary scrutiny from relevant departments, and then in the absence of a single supporting department channelled it to ERWG for decision. At the 2 July meeting the idea was endorsed in principle. InvestHK was given the limited specific follow-up assignment of scrutinising the budget. There was no directive to consider alternative forms of financing. If ERWG had wanted such an examination it could easily have requested one. It did not do so and its members should carry responsibility for this failure. Yet use of the words "submitted to the ERWG for consideration" gives the impression that InvestHK's role had somehow grown backwards in time to include evaluation of the project and consideration of alternative forms of financing *before* the 2 July meeting.

ONCE THE REPORT had lost the thread, the critique of HarbourFest and of InvestHK's role became seriously flawed.

Having apparently accepted that HarbourFest was an Am-

Cham project which the ERWG had wrongly decided the Government should sponsor only, the report elsewhere treats the event as a Government project with AmCham as the selected implementation agent. This error is most marked in paragraph 3.2 of the report:

> In view of the large sum of public money involved and the fact that it was an innovative project entrusted to an organiser without a proven track record, it was still necessary for the Government to establish an effective monitoring mechanism to ensure that the project would be implemented as planned.

The report then goes on to make a number of criticisms. In so far as they are valid, and many of them are, they are valid as criticisms of the decision that the Government should be a "sponsor only". The Director in paragraph 3.5 refers to the spirit of Stores and Procurement Regulations in the context of engagement of artists. But for HarbourFest the Government did not engage any artists, AmCham did. So the criticism is valid only if the Government had been the organiser, or at least co-organiser.

Having set off down the wrong path, the report arrives by paragraph 3.8 at a re-write of history:

> In the case of the Harbour Fest, InvestHK was designated to be the subject department for scrutinising the proposal and taking up the project. Therefore, the DGIP had a specific role to play as the Controlling Officer of the subject department identified for taking up the Harbour Fest project.

THE CRUX OF THE ISSUE was this: from the perspective of InvestHK and commercial organisations in most cases, a sponsorship deal is one where an organiser offers a package of benefits which could take various forms (title sponsorship where the name of the sponsor company/organisation is included in the name of the event itself e.g. a tennis tournament; prominent display of company logo at the venue; page(s) of advertising in event programme; ability to provide a speaker in a prominent time slot of a conference etc).

The potential sponsor compares the package with the requested sponsorship fee, and decides whether or not in marketing terms it is worthwhile to go ahead. As far as the sponsor is concerned, his money is considered "spent" when the agreed fee is handed over to the organiser. His concern from that point on is not with how the organiser in turn spends the money, but rather with ensuring that the package of promised benefits is delivered.

In the case of HarbourFest, ERWG had made the decision that it was worthwhile for the Government to sponsor the event. But because the Audit Director struggled to accept that the Government had decided to be a "sponsor only" (he was right to struggle, but that was the decision of ERWG as the minutes clearly showed) he used words and constructions to imply the department was responsible for how the money was spent by the organiser.

By this bureaucratic sleight of hand, I had become the Controlling Officer for HarbourFest itself.

"Independent" Panel of Inquiry

ON 5 NOVEMBER 2003, FS Henry Tang announced that the Chief Executive would appoint an independent panel of inquiry to investigate the Harbour Fest event. The two-man Panel, consisting of Moses Cheng and Brian Stevenson, was subsequently appointed on 12 December.

The timing of the announcement was no coincidence. On Wednesdays when Hong Kong's Legislative Council is in session, Members have 20 opportunities to put questions to the Administration, rather like Prime Minister's Question Time in the U.K. House of Commons but with responsibility for answering falling to the Minister responsible for that subject. Normally the first six questions are put orally, and supplementary questions are permitted. The Secretary concerned (i.e. Minister) reads out a prepared answer to the main question but must then answer any supplementary questions as best he can, thinking on his feet. The remaining 14 questions are asked and answered in writing, and there is no opportunity for supplementary questions.

Clearly, the oral questions are much harder to cope with than written ones and much preparation work goes into trying to anticipate possible supplementaries. Reflecting public concern about Harbour Fest, no fewer than four of the six oral questions put down for 5 November were about the event, the first time in the history of Hong Kong there had been such focus on a single subject.

IN PREPARATION FOR the LegCo session Tang convened meetings of the key officials involved to discuss how best to answer the HarbourFest questions.

It was at this point that the absence of a clearly identified Minister came once again into play. There was no alternative: the FS as Minister for the overall relaunch campaign would have to answer the questions himself.

The announcement of the proposed establishment of an independent panel was a key element of the Government's overall response. The hope was that Members would be satisfied that the Administration was taking the subject seriously and would conduct a thorough-going investigation. The Permanent Secretary for Commerce, Industry and Technology, Denise Yue, queried the advisability of creating such a body bearing in mind that once the panel was established the Administration might lose control of the process. "What is the end game here?" she asked. Another relevant question might have been "If you really want to get to the bottom of things, why not appoint a fully fledged Commission of Inquiry, headed by a High Court Judge?"

The answer to both questions became apparent when the CE, on the recommendation of the FS, announced the appointments. The two appointees were well respected in their respective professions, Cheng as senior partner of a prominent local solicitors firm, Stevenson as a former president of the Hong Kong Society of Accountants, so the Panel could plausibly be described as qualified and competent.

But both Cheng and Stevenson were close associates of Henry Tang. Cheng and Tang had been co-founders of the Cooperative Resources Centre, a loose grouping of LegCo Members that was to be a forerunner of the Liberal Party. Stevenson and Tang had been fellow Stewards of the Hong Kong Jockey Club, a small but elite group. So by ruling out a proper Commission of Inquiry (which would have meant hearings held in public, legal representation, cross-examination of witnesses etc), and recommending two of his close associates to the CE for appointment, the Government in the person of the FS in fact kept control. The addition of the word "Independent" to the Panel's title is perhaps an example of PR spin at its finest.

The FS also asked me to accompany him to LegCo that afternoon to sit behind him. "I need you there," Tang said. "You are my lightning conductor".

And so it proved. As Tang ducked and weaved before the Council and the TV cameras, every implied inadequacy in the Administration's performance could in the viewer's mind be laid at my door. After something of an ordeal, the Government limped out of LegCo battered and bruised, but ultimately saved by the shield of the promised "Independent" Panel.

THE TWO-MAN PANEL got down to work after the 12 December announcement. Proceedings were well resourced, with full-time administrative support and a secretary of court stenographer standard. This meant that every day there was a draft transcript of what had been said which after tidying up could also be shown to the witnesses, inviting their corrections, additions, clarifications and so on.

In my evidence to the Panel, I made clear what we in InvestHK understood by sponsorship, that is, payment of an agreed fee for an agreed set of benefits. We had accepted the role of Government agent for HarbourFest on this basis and this basis alone. It was the basis upon which we had sponsored many events before, and had continued to sponsor many events since HarbourFest. If any other basis had been intended, then we could not have accepted the role and another department should have been selected.

When asked why we had not sought the right of access to the detailed accounts of HarbourFest, my reply was that we never did. For example, when we sponsored the Fortune Global Forum (2001) or the Forbes Global CEO Conference (2002), our focus was on ensuring that we received in full the promised benefits, e.g. number and seniority of attending businessmen, number and prominence of InvestHK advertisements, names and contact details of attendees, ability to place marketing materials in delegates' bags etc. Questions such as how much the organisers paid the speakers, which hotels they put them up in, what class of air travel they received etc. were matters for the organisers. Similarly, with the two soccer matches sponsored as part of the relaunch campaign (local representative teams played against Liverpool and the David Beckham-led Real Madrid), we were interested only in whether the teams turned up and fielded their star players, not in the amount of their match fees.

Scrutiny of detailed accounts was a matter for the organiser or co-organisers as the case may be. But as in the case of HarbourFest we had been directed to be a "sponsor only", our interest in the accounts was limited to ensuring that they were properly audited so that the fee could be capped at $100 million or such lesser amount as might be justified.

MY COLLEAGUES Ophelia Tsang and David Chiu were also interviewed by the Panel. Unusually, they were interviewed together instead of separately, and not given an opportunity to supplement their brief oral evidence. This failure was to become apparent at the disciplinary hearings later, when it seriously, albeit temporarily, embarrassed the prosecution.

The Panel's report, when it came (submitted to CE 15 May, published on 17 May) was similar in many respects to the Audit Report, although in some areas it went further. Cheng and Stevenson flat out rejected our interpretation of sponsorship even though it had been practised for many years before (and since), and apparently invented their own interpretation the standards of which they then claimed I and the department had failed to meet.

The Panel also came very close to making me the Controlling Officer for HarbourFest in paragraph 29 of its report, which implies strongly that I remained responsible for how AmCham spent the $100 million sponsorship fee even after we had handed it over as instructed by ERWG. In paragraph 40, the Panel recommended that the Government should in future be represented on the organising committee of similar events, i.e. be a co-organiser. But this term was not used in the Panel's report, because it would have placed responsibility for the perceived shortcomings of the Government's handling firmly on the shoulders of the body which had made the original "sponsor only" decision: ERWG, now chaired of course by their colleague Henry Tang.

Public Accounts Committee

THE PUBLIC ACCOUNTS COMMITTEE (PAC) comprises seven Members of the Legislative Council. Their job is to scrutinise reports prepared by the Director of Audit and follow up on those where they believe the Government has not deployed public funds appropriately and/or has not achieved value for money. In the case of HarbourFest, the PAC held public hearings on 3, 7, 18 and 20 May 2004. It also took into account the report of the "Independent" Panel before publishing its own report in June.

Where the Director of Audit had unlocked the door, and the "Independent" Panel had opened it, PAC marched boldly through. Once again the instruction from ERWG to be a "sponsor only" was interpreted as meaning I should be a co-organiser and my many failures in this regard spelled out.

The PAC was helped in its journey towards this conclusion by three key answers given by FS Henry Tang.

Tang had caused a new Financial Circular to be issued in February 2004. It dealt with the responsibilities of Controlling Officers (i.e. vote holders) under Hong Kong's Public Finance Ordinance. Its reference number was FC 1/2004 and it replaced FC 14/1984 which covered similar – but not identical – ground.

The new circular said that its purpose was "to *remind* Controlling Officers of their responsibilities" [emphasis added] and read in part:

> Irrespective of whether public funds are disbursed through a
> procurement contract, subvention, sponsorship, or any other
> form of vehicle, Controlling Officers should satisfy themselves

that an appropriate system of cost control or monitoring is in place, having regard to economy, efficiency and effectiveness in the delivery of public service and use of public funds.

From the words "Controlling Officers" onwards, the statement is entirely reasonable.

However, since this was the first ever reference to sponsorship in this context, it is clear that the circular is retroactive. Moreover, the inclusion of the phrase "Irrespective of ... vehicle" makes it nonsensical, for taken literally, the revised wording is simply unworkable.

It seems to imply that any person or organisation which is to receive public funds in whatever manner must have a system of cost-control in place and the Controlling Officer who hands over the public funds must satisfy himself on this point. If the Government decides to purchase cars after a competitive tender exercise, does the CO need to satisfy himself that the vehicle dealer concerned has a proper system of cost control? That surely would be superfluous, as the procurement process itself is a safeguard.

In the context of sponsorship, the questions are even more numerous. For a major event like the HK Rugby 7s tournament, there may be one or two title sponsors putting in a significant sum of money (in recent years, Cathay Pacific and a major bank) plus a large number of smaller ones paying only a small amount. While it is reasonable for the major sponsors to secure a place on the organising committee to monitor closely both expenditure and operations – effectively thereby becoming co-organisers – it would become unmanageable for the minor sponsors to do the same. The question is directly relevant to InvestHK because it has been a minor sponsor of the Rugby 7s for several years.

It might well have been reasonable, given the scale of the Government support for HarbourFest, for ERWG to require as a condition of approval that the Government be a co-organiser and given a place on the organising committee. But in the heat of the moment, it chose not to do so.

Leaving aside procurement issues, which are dealt with adequately elsewhere in Government Regulations dealing with Stores and Procurement, perhaps what the circular was trying to do was say that the degree of Government involvement in monitoring should be commensurate with the scale of Government funding. Where the Government was providing a significant percentage of the budget, it should be a co-organiser rather than a sponsor.

Tang was asked by the Committee whether there was any difference between the two circulars and paragraph 47 of the PAC report provides his response: "no difference between the requirements in these two circulars" and "irrespective of whether an event was financed by the Government through sponsorship or other modes of subvention, the responsibilities of the Controlling Officers remained the same i.e. they should satisfy themselves that an appropriate system of cost control or monitoring was in place."

Later, when answering a question about monitoring, the FS quoted the wording of the new circular (which was not prevailing at the time of HarbourFest) as part of his reply

> as the Controlling Officer for the $1 billion relaunch fund, the DGIP had the responsibility to properly monitor the use of the fund, irrespective of whether the fund was disbursed through sponsorship or other modes of subvention. [Paragraph 61 of the report]

Just in case there was still any doubt about who Tang thought should be carrying the can, his answer in response to another question read

> The Financial Secretary responded that given that $100 million was a huge sum amounting to 10% of the $1 billion relaunch fund, the Government had the duty to monitor *how it was used*, irrespective of whether the HarbourFest was a commissioned or

sponsored event. [Paragraph 96, emphasis added]

The lightning conductor had clearly served his purpose and could now be safely discarded.

The Committee, under the chairmanship of Eric Li, felt sufficiently strongly by the time it got to paragraph 120 of its report to "condemn" DGIP and

> urge(s) the Administration to consider taking disciplinary action against the DGIP, having regard to the gravity of his failure in discharging his duties.

So there it was, all out frontal assault.[1]

WHAT BEGAN as a mistake by ERWG in deciding to be a "sponsor only" of an AmCham event has now been transformed into a mistake by the person who implemented the decision, by pretending that HarbourFest had become a Government event with AmCham as the subvented organisation responsible for delivering it. It's not a new tactic: it's called "moving the goalposts".

Civil Service Proceedings

ARTICLE 48 of the Basic Law empowers the Chief Executive (CE) to make Executive Orders. The Public Service (Administration) Order was the first such order made by the Special Administrative Region Government after 1997. It was made in 2000 and deals with the hiring and management of the civil service. Charges of Misconduct may be brought against a civil servant under Section 9 (for cases not deemed sufficiently serious to warrant dismissal) or Section 10 (for cases deemed sufficiently serious as to possibly warrant dismissal). Section 21 of the Order empowers the CE to make Regulations governing how the cases are handled.

Although this all sounds reasonably fresh and modern, the philosophy behind the Order and the Regulations derives directly from the previous arrangements that applied before 1 July 1997, when Hong Kong was under British Administration. Moreover, those arrangements in turn seem to have changed relatively little since they were first devised at the height of the British Empire in the 19th century.

In brief, the Secretary for the Civil Service (SCS) has the power to decide whether charges should be brought, what the charges should be, and whether they should be brought under Section 9 or 10. He employs the prosecutor and selects the judges (the Inquiry Committee). Under delegated power from the CE, he has power of veto over the "Friend" who can assist the defendant. At the end of the trial stage, he decides whether or not to accept the findings of the Inquiry Committee. And finally he determines the penalty, albeit after seeking the views of the Public Service Commission.

In other words, all relevant power is concentrated in the hands of a single individual.

ON 3 SEPTEMBER 2004, the Civil Service Bureau invited me to state why a disciplinary inquiry should not be held. I replied on 18 September to the effect that yet another inquiry into HarbourFest would not teach us anything else we did not know already, all necessary lessons had been taken on board, and we should all now get on with our substantive jobs.

On 5 October, I was informed that then SCS Joseph Wong Wing Ping had given approval for a Section 10 disciplinary inquiry to be brought against me. There were five charges and I indicated I would plead not guilty to all of them.

Bearing in mind that I potentially faced dismissal with loss of all pension benefits, I decided to engage a law firm to help me fight the charges. On 20 October, Messrs Herbert Smith sought permission from the CE to represent me in the hearings. This application was in accordance with a provision in the Regulations which allowed me to be represented by a "Friend" who could be any civil servant other than a qualified lawyer, or "such other person as the CE may allow". It turned out that the power to determine such applications had been delegated by the CE to SCS (the very guy who had decided to prosecute me in the first place) and I was informed on 3 November – just 9 days before the trial was due to start – that SCS had rejected my request.

THE SEARCH FOR a Friend was instructive. From among the large number of senior retired officials with whom I had previously worked I approached several who I had thought of as personal friends, either of myself or my wife, not just ex-colleagues. All turned me down with one exception, my colleague John Wan (who, due to similarities in appearance and aspects of personal behaviour, was often known as my "brother"). One other former colleague – Liz Bosher – approached me on her own initiative to offer help. They were the only two who showed the courage to fight the system which was determined to do something blatantly unfair.

While I was still mulling over which of these two brave souls to bring in to the firing line alongside me, I attended an official lunch hosted by one of the chambers of commerce and found myself seated next to a former LegCo Member Christine Loh. She asked why I was so pensive and I explained.

More in hope than expectation, I then threw out a casual invitation "I don't suppose you would be interested in acting for me?" Much to my surprise – and delight – Loh instantly agreed.

Like just about everyone else in Hong Kong Government and political circles, I had a high regard for Loh's intelligence, energy and resolve to improve our community in every respect with a special focus on the environment. After stepping down from LegCo she had established a high profile think-tank called Civic-Exchange which carried out and published studies on important issues of the day.

It had not seriously occurred to me that she would have the inclination or the time to devote the necessary weeks on research and preparation for the actual hearing days. I decided that the gentlemanly thing to do would be to offer her a ladder to climb down if she had had second thoughts. So the next day I e-mailed her explaining that I already had two volunteers and if on examining her diary she realised it would be too much of a commitment to take on my case then I would quite understand if she wished to withdraw.

Christine Loh – miles ahead of me as usual in grasping the full constitutional implications of what was happening – crisply confirmed her previous willingness. I promptly applied to CSB for approval and they equally promptly agreed. There had been a doubt in my mind whether the Administration would be willing because Loh was and is a political heavyweight. In parallel, I thanked John and Liz for their support and sought their understanding of my choice.

It proved to be an inspired one. Although Loh is not legally qualified, which would have rendered her ineligible under CSB policy, she is legally trained and therefore adopts the kind of structured thinking process which was to prove invaluable as the case progressed.

In the meantime, SCS had selected then Judiciary Administrator Wilfred Tsui as chairman of the Inquiry Committee and then Permanent Secretary for Environment, Transport and Works Y C Lo as the second member. A Senior Principal Executive Officer in the Secretariat on Civil Service Discipline Rupert Cheung was the chosen "Assisting Officer". The wording of these various titles is interesting. The Inquiry Committee is supposed to be impartial and fair-minded (whether the supposition was borne out in this case is something readers will no doubt judge for themselves later) and the Assisting Officer is supposed to support them in similar vein. In fact he acts as the prosecutor and his mission is to nail your hide to the floor. This contradiction almost guarantees an unfair result, as it is common for the "Assisting Officer", i.e. prosecutor, to help in drafting the Inquiry Committee's final report.

THE INQUIRY COMMITTEE held 12 sessions on a series of dates between 12 November 2004 and 22 January 2005. The IC heard oral evidence from four prosecution witnesses (Lawrence Wong, Senior Assistant Law Officer of the Department of Justice; Ophelia Tsang, one of my deputies at InvestHK; David Chiu, one of the team leaders at InvestHK; and Financial Secretary Henry Tang); and one defence witness (myself).

The first session on 12 November largely dealt with housekeeping and procedural matters. The process that would be followed was set out by the chairman. The charges were put to me and formally denied. The prosecutor then put forward his version of the case background. This was supposed to be a fairly neutral factual description but we found it so prejudicial that Loh was later to submit a written commentary on it. Both versions were included in the IC's final report.

Two major issues were broached at this session. They were the question of whether the previous Financial Secretary Antony

Leung could and should appear as a witness, and our request for timely accurate transcripts.

On the first matter, my solicitors had written to CSB on 3 November asking that Leung be called. The prosecutor had included extracts from his statement to the Panel of Inquiry as evidence in these proceedings and we therefore wanted to cross-examine him on those remarks. CSB had invited Leung to appear but he had declined. We were advised that there were no powers to subpoena witnesses even where their presence was critical to a fair hearing.

This was a very serious matter. In Leung's evidence to the Panel, which the prosecutor was attempting to admit in the disciplinary hearing, he claimed that the directive to InvestHK to examine the budget for HarbourFest meant we were supposed to conduct a full-scale bottom up review of the whole idea, i.e. treating it as a fresh proposal for evaluation. Such an outrageous and self-serving re-write of history had gone unchallenged by the Panel (on the contrary, Cheng and Stevenson seemed very much of the same view) but it was going to be vigorously challenged by us.

In the circumstances, Tsui had no alternative but to rule that the extracts could not be used as supporting evidence in the discipline case. But in reality the damage had already been done, because Leung's evidence had undoubtedly affected the Panel's findings and later influenced the PAC. And no doubt it lingered in the mind of the Inquiry Committee too.

The second issue on transcripts was an attempt to work around the refusal by SCS to let me be legally represented. If the best we could do was brief the lawyers on a daily basis on what had taken place and then get their advice on what lines to pursue the next hearing day, then obviously we needed as accurate as possible a record of proceedings. In other words, we were looking for the same level of administrative support as had been given to the Panel of Inquiry and in particular daily verbatim transcripts. Tsui agreed to refer our request to CSB but it was quickly rejected on the grounds of lack of resources. We were instead offered tape recordings. However when it transpired that the quality of the tapes was for the most part very poor (professional transcription services found whole sessions virtually inaudible), I offered to pay for top quality secretarial support myself, and let both the prosecution and the Inquiry Committee have copies. This offer too was rejected. The lack of contemporaneous transcripts seriously handicapped the defence team.

FIRST "PROSECUTION" WITNESS Wong gave evidence at the second session on 30 November. His evidence for the most part was unremarkable. In response to a specific question from me he confirmed that if he had had any serious reservations about the final draft of the contract with AmCham, he would have set out those reservations in writing to protect his own professional reputation. However he had no such reservations. This was significant because a number of the charges against me revolved around alleged deficiencies in the contract.

Tsang began her evidence on 1 December and concluded it at a second session on 7 December. Chiu gave his evidence on 7 and 8 December. Both gave detailed evidence about how InvestHK had monitored the progress of the preparations for HarbourFest.

Although they were nominally prosecution witnesses, much of their evidence in fact refuted large swathes of the charges. Chiu for example produced 14 pages of detailed calculations which had been forwarded by AmCham in early July to substantiate the budget estimates. He had not been given the opportunity to present this evidence to the Panel of Inquiry in the brief joint session with Tsang. And as he had not been given the opportunity later to comment on the record of his oral evidence, he had not had the chance to introduce it subsequently either.

In his mind the budget broke down into two broad areas: artist fees which could not be checked because there had been no negotiations with any artists by early July so the provisional sum which represented about 70% of the total budget could only be noted, and the 30% relating to production costs which could be broken down and scrutinised – and were, by examining the 14 pages of detail which he had done.

The prosecutor and the Inquiry Committee were shocked by this evidence because it completely destroyed the first charge against me. The prosecutor was unsighted because he had relied on the Panel of Inquiry report and had failed to question in advance his own witness. At the discipline hearing he simply asked Chiu to confirm that he was satisfied with the record of his evidence to the Panel, and we were all surprised when Chiu replied "No, not entirely". When asked for clarification, he explained about the lack of opportunity to tell the Panel about the 14 pages. The Inquiry Committee was momentarily stunned. (Tsui flipped through the pages murmuring things like "But it's all here, ... even the number of water bottles and chairs").

In the event, the Committee's final report made no mention of the 14 pages. Perhaps in the 66 pages of the main report and 24 pages of annexures there was insufficient space. Or perhaps the evidence was just too inconvenient.

CHIU ALSO CHALLENGED one of the basic premises under which the IC was working.

> All of your questions are from the point of view of how to save money. But the whole purpose of economic relaunch was not to save money. It was to spend money to save the economy.

There were several key points on which both Tsang and Chiu agreed: they did not know at the time, and still did not know more than one year later, who had been the Minister for HarbourFest; the only sum mentioned in ERWG for the sponsorship fee was $100 million: no-one had ever mentioned a lower figure; the only relationship the Government contemplated was one of sponsor, no-one had floated the possible alternatives of organiser or co-organiser; and no-one had queried the choice of InvestHK as the department to implement the sponsorship arrangement.

THE EVIDENCE of the first three prosecution witnesses then was pretty straightforward and exculpatory rather than damning. Everything would depend on Henry Tang. His first appearance was bizarre.

The FS' job is one of the busiest in the Government and getting a one-hour slot in his diary is hard at the best of times. Getting one or two full days, which is what we thought might be needed, seemed unlikely but we all agreed to take it one session at a time. The first slot the IC secured was the afternoon of 6 December. Even though Tsang had not completed her evidence on 1 December, we (prosecution and defence) agreed to make best use of the half-day by allowing the prosecutor to skip ahead to his next witness rather than losing part of the time by wrapping up Tsang's testimony.

Shortly after 2pm, Tang entered the conference room where the hearing was taking place, bringing with him his Administrative Assistant Shirley Yuen. As the room cleared of the various CSB support personnel, Tsui noticed there was an extra body present and asked who she was: "I'm afraid I don't know the lady".

When Tang explained she was there to help him give evidence by locating relevant documents he might wish to refer to, Tsui paused and said this was unusual as this was supposed to be a closed session. He needed to adjourn briefly to seek advice. Tang and Yuen left the room together and Tsui asked me for my reaction. By chance I had half suspected that given the closeness of the relationships that inevitably developed between the top officials and their AAs such an eventuality might materialise and had sought legal advice. The view of Herbert Smith was that this would constitute a "material irregularity".

On hearing this expression Tsui turned pale. Although I did not know it at the time, he was preparing to become a barrister in private practice and understood the full legal significance of these words: they could potentially render the entire proceedings null and void.

The chairman promptly adjourned. Loh and I were ushered to an adjacent room and asked to wait. It seemed highly likely that the next ten minutes were used to obtain legal advice, though as the Department of Justice was later to claim that it had never given advice to the Inquiry Committee itself, only to CSB, the advice was presumably given to the Assisting Officer.

We reconvened at 2.20pm but there was no Tang. When he had not returned by 2.30, Tsui adjourned again. We resumed at 2.38. Prosecutor Cheung reported that Tang still wished to have his AA with him to help him give evidence and if he could not have her, he would need longer to prepare himself. Tsui advised that nothing in the procedures permitted this, moreover I had objected on legal advice. I gently corrected him: I had not objected, merely reported to him the legal advice I had been given; the decision on whether or not to allow the duo to give evidence together rested with him.

The chairman said Tang could be told that the proceedings would move slowly and the IC would help him find the relevant documents. The prosecutor said Tang appreciated this, but none-theless would not be returning that day without Yuen.

Stalemate. Loh expressed variously astonishment and "extreme disappointment" at the turn of events.

After wrapping up a few administrative and procedural points, the IC adjourned for the day at 3.15. Tang did not return to give evidence for over a month.

IT WAS NOT until 10 and 11 January 2005 that it was possible to get all parties together again for the purpose of securing evidence from the FS. The prosecutor kept things simple and basically asked the FS to confirm the various written replies he had given to written questions put to him by CSB in the run up to the case.

Of the 43 questions put to him in July and August 2004, Tang had referred to the findings/conclusions of the Panel of Inquiry no fewer than 15 times. In effect, therefore, he was being allowed to adopt the findings of the Panel as his own evidence. Bearing in mind that those findings were based on evidence not given under oath and not subject to cross-examination, this was unfair in the extreme.

In the discipline proceedings, of course, cross-examination was allowed and Loh challenged him on this point.

Loh: In reply to CSB, why did you not give your own opinion? You kept referring to what was in the independent panel report.

Tang: Because the Government, the Chief Executive had invited the panel to look into the Harbour Fest affair, and they have produced a report, and the government has accepted the findings of the report. So, as a member of the government, I am bound by – the government has accepted the findings of the report.

Loh: Okay. Based on your own knowledge rather than relying on the report, are you aware of any instances where Mr Rowse's conduct could be described as improper?

Tang: No.

Loh: Have you ever advocated that Mr Rowse should have disciplinary proceedings brought against him?

Tang: No.

I GAVE EVIDENCE, was cross-examined and re-examined over three days in January. The prosecutor summed up, Loh summed up on my behalf, and the IC adjourned to consider its verdict.

I will briefly outline the charges and our defence here, but would also refer readers to the full set of charges and the complete defence submission at *www.rowse.com.hk*.

Charge A said that I had failed to adequately examine Am-Cham's draft budget for HarbourFest, as I had been instructed to do by the ERWG meeting on 2 July, prior to reconsideration at its next meeting on 12 July. However the evidence (mainly from the prosecution's own witnesses) showed that the portion of the budget which could be critically examined had been, and that the remainder could at that stage only have been a "best guess". Moreover the paper put to ERWG on the second occasion made clear that the budget was preliminary only.

Charge B criticised the Memoranda of Understanding whereby interim payments had been passed to AmCham, for failing to protect the Government's interests in a number of respects. However, the evidence (again, largely from the prosecution witnesses) was that all the things necessary to protect the Government were in practice being done, and that without these interim payments the whole event could not have proceeded.

Charge C alleged the same deficiencies in the final contract, and our defence was essentially the same as for Charge B.

Charge D accused me of failing to ensure AmCham conducted a critical review of ticket pricing, and also threw in a separate point about distribution of free tickets. Our defence was that not only had there been such a review, the outcome of it was actually included as an annex to the contract with AmCham, and as a result of the review, revenue from ticket sales had increased from the initial estimate of $11 million to over $48 million. The free tickets were either the consequence of unforeseen circumstances (e.g. sudden non-availability of lead artist) or were a marketing tactic which fell within the discretion of the organiser.

Charge E alleged I had failed to establish proper procedures to monitor the event, thereby prejudicing the Government's interests. The defence was that there had been procedures and there had been monitoring and the Government's interests had not been prejudiced.

LOH'S 54-PAGE SUBMISSION was a masterpiece of research and intellectual rigour. It not only cast doubt on the prosecution case, it completely destroyed, line by line, each charge. All to no avail. On 4 February, the IC produced its report finding me guilty or partly guilty on all five charges.

There are so many errors and so much faulty logic in the report that it would be tedious to list them out, let alone explain them in full. I will content myself with a single example. Readers will recall that HarbourFest was an AmCham initiative which ERWG had decided the Government should sponsor. Yet paragraph 84 of the IC's report portrayed HarbourFest as an InvestHK initiative with AmCham as our project organisers. The world had truly turned upside down.

Even CSB had reservations about some of the findings and after a pause wrote to the IC on 12 April to seek clarification of certain aspects. For example, on Charge E the IC had found there was no evidence to show the Government's interests had been prejudiced, yet had still found me partly guilty. The reply from Tsui one week later did not shed any new light, for the most part simply referring back to sections of the original report. On 12 May, I was advised that SCS had accepted the findings in full.

THE NEXT FIVE MONTHS were taken up with the penalty phase and on 3 October I was informed that the punishment would be "a severe reprimand and a fine equivalent to reduction in salary by two increments for twelve months" (i.e. about one month's pay) and a caution that in the event of further misconduct, serious consideration would be given to removing me from the service. All things considered, this was a very mild penalty given the gravity of the charges.

The Appeal

MY FIRST APPEAL against SCS' decision to accept the findings of the Inquiry Committee was dated 10 June 2005 and was addressed to Wong himself asking him to reconsider his earlier decision. Just one week later, the prosecutor (not exactly the most unbiased party, one would have thought) replied to this appeal saying that it was considered inappropriate for SCS to consider it and advising that I should instead address any appeal to the Chief Executive.

There then followed several months of correspondence dealing with the question of penalty, and I was informed of SCS' final decision (after consulting the Public Service Commission) on 3 October.

On 13 October 2005, I appealed to the Chief Executive under Section 20 of the Public Service (Administration) Order against SCS' decision to accept the findings of the Inquiry Committee. This appeal was referred by the Chief Executive's Office back to CSB! Fully three months later, on 13 January 2006, I was provided with a copy of the CSB comments on my appeal and invited to make submissions to the Office of the Chief Executive in relation to those comments, which I duly did on 19 January.

Nothing then happened for over a year, although there were reports in a local newspaper shortly afterwards that the CE had delegated responsibility for handling the appeal to then Chief Secretary Rafael Hui. These reports later turned out to be true. It also turned out that the act of delegation was itself unlawful, but that only emerged later.

Although no substantive response to the petition was received for over 15 months, the issue did not disappear from public consciousness. On the contrary, the case was raised twice in the Legislative Council. On 24 May 2006, Audrey Eu tabled an oral question to the Secretary for the Civil Service querying progress of the disciplinary case and determination of my appeal. The question fell to be answered by Denise Yue who had taken over from Joseph Wong as SCS the previous year.

The time taken to deal with the question, including supplementaries, was relatively long at over 21 minutes. It emerged that the average time taken to deal with such appeals was 2-3 months. Yue tried her best to explain why my case was taking so long (around eight months by that time), using expressions like "complicated", "particularly complicated", "extremely complicated", "exceptional", and "extremely special". By 20 December, Eu raised the question again, this time in writing. Clearly, the issue was going to become embroiled in the campaign for the CE election, due to take place in the first half of 2007.

ON FRIDAY 31 JANUARY 2007, my office received a phone call from the Chief Secretary's Office checking my movements later that day and advising that an important letter would be delivered before 5pm. After that phone call, but before arrival of the letter, a reporter from Apple Daily was on the phone checking my whereabouts. Shortly before 5pm the letter arrived. It advised that the CE had delegated his power to deal with the appeal to the CS, and that the CS had rejected my appeal, upholding the decision of SCS to accept the findings of the Inquiry Committee.

It had been a point of pride with me throughout all the years of the HarbourFest disciplinary proceedings to maintain in full my schedule of official duties. As I had a function that evening to welcome a new foreign investor, I left the office shortly after receiving the CS' letter and attended the cocktail reception which was closed to the media.

Upon return to the office later that evening, a reporter and a photographer from Apple Daily were waiting for me in the downstairs lift lobby and travelled up with me in the lift to the floor where InvestHK's offices were located. "What is your reaction to the letter" the reporter wanted to know.

"Has there been an official statement?" I asked by way of reply.

"No," he said.

"Fine," I said. "When there is an official statement, there will be an official response."

I WAS NOT AT ALL surprised that news of the letter and its contents had been leaked to the media as there had been many examples of planted stories during the saga. But it was interesting that those concerned had used Apple Daily this time. It had been more common in the past to use another media group. Perhaps the parties concerned were being clever and trying to cover their tracks.

But the complete lack of reaction on my part must have caused some consternation (my reply did not even confirm or deny there had been any letter, let alone the contents) so several newspapers were then approached and told – falsely – that I had spoken about the result of my appeal at a public function that evening. These papers in turn contacted the Government Information Services where the Duty Officer had an "In response to Enquiries" statement ready.

On this occasion the dirty tricks backfired. Because I had said nothing of substance on the record on Friday evening, the papers on Saturday carried the story of CS rejecting my appeal in moderate coverage but could not include my response because there had not been one. When we issued a strongly worded statement at noon on Saturday making clear that I would pursue the matter further, this became a separate – and much bigger – story in its own right. It was very prominent in the electronic media for the rest of the day, and the front page lead in the Sunday Morning Post the next day.

IT WAS ABOUT this time that the media coverage of the whole

HarbourFest/discipline story began to swing to a more neutral, and then even more sympathetic, tone.

Up to now I had been the villain who had unwisely wasted $100 million of the public's money. Suddenly I was transformed into the underdog preparing to take on powerful forces single-handed. When I was seen as part of the Government, I could do no right.

When I was seen as being against the Government, I became something of an unlikely hero.

Judicial Review

THE STAGE WAS now set for the final confrontation: Judicial Review (JR) of the disciplinary process.

It took us some time to work out who we should be taking legal action against and on what grounds. Our first inclination was to go after the Inquiry Committee which had reached several conclusions which were manifestly wrong. But Messrs Herbert Smith correctly deduced that the IC was not "the decision maker". That person had been Joseph Wong when as SCS he decided to accept the findings of the IC. Those findings were, in our submission, so flawed that he should not have accepted them. So we would seek a JR of that decision.

Then we had appealed to the CE. Our reading of the law – subsequently upheld – was that the CE needed to deal with the appeal himself and was precluded from delegating it to someone else. He had however decided to pass the appeal to the CS. That was the second decision which we would ask the court to review.

And finally there was CS Hui's decision to reject the appeal on behalf of CE. Leaving aside the fact that the delegation to him was itself unlawful, for the same reasons as SCS should have not accepted the IC's findings, Hui should have rejected them also and upheld the appeal. Those were the three key decisions in respect of which we sought a judicial review and we put forward a number of arguments in support of our case.

TO THE UNINITIATED, the whole process of JR must seem extraordinary. In the first place, there are no live witnesses at the actual hearing, all the arguments are on the basis of Affidavits prepared beforehand and filed with the court and given to the opposing party. Moreover, even before the hearing, each side must set out in writing the arguments they will be raising, and pass copies to the other side and file them with the court. This document is called the "skeleton".

You may wonder what there would be left to argue about, and assume the proceedings would be rather dry and boring. They were anything but.

Secondly, and perhaps more fundamentally, the court is not acting as a general court of appeal in such cases. It is, rather, sitting in a supervisory capacity reviewing the decision-making process. That said, in practice it is inevitable that a JR will have to refer to the underlying case itself, at least to an extent.

WE FILED FOR JR on the afternoon of 16 April 2007, mine being the only Affidavit in support of the application. It was considered by a judge of the High Court, Mr Justice Hartmann, a man well-respected in legal circles for the compelling logic of his decisions (which were seldom successfully appealed) and with a reputation for fairness.

I had been advised that it could take around two weeks for the court to examine the grounds on which we were seeking approval to proceed and decide which if any of them were at least arguable. In the event, we received the Judge's written approval to proceed with all our grounds just three days later on the morning of 19 April.

The next day we served notice on the three Respondents. Four Government officials filed their affidavits in June in response. The four were Chief Secretary Rafael Hui, Private Secretary to the Chief Executive Jessie Yip, Secretary for the Civil Service Joseph Wong, and a Law Officer in the Department of Justice Ian Wingfield.

We had decided that I would be represented by a QC from London who specialised in administrative and human rights law, by the name of Richard Gordon. His junior would be a HK based counsel called Alex Stock, son of an Appeal Court Judge. It took some time to obtain the Bar Association's approval to bring Gordon in. The Government meanwhile had decided to brief out the case to a Senior Counsel in private practice, Joseph Fok.

The two sides agreed we would need at least three days for hearing the case and should allow a reserve day. It proved difficult to find a slot where everyone's diary could accommodate four consecutive days and the hearing was finally set for 24-26 February 2008, with 27 in reserve. In the event, proceedings took up the whole week. The fireworks may have taken a long time to arrive, but the show did not disappoint once it had started.

DAY 1 WAS TAKEN UP by my counsel ploughing steadily through the skeleton argument, amplifying and expanding on the various points we had put forward. He had an interesting technique which baffled me at first but which I came to appreciate as the hearing progressed. Simply put, Gordon would present the argument comprehensively and compellingly and then right at the end not articulate the final conclusion. It was like telling a joke and then, just when everybody could see the point and was waiting for the punch line as a trigger to burst out laughing, he would stop. I realised after some hours of listening to this just how effective the technique could be. In effect, he was doing the donkey work of the "joke", then leaving it to the judge to deliver the only possible punch line.

The highlight of the first day was his recitation of a series of emails dealing with the minutes of a meeting. On 31 October 2003, the Economic Relaunch Working Group had taken stock of the situation on HarbourFest and the Financial Secretary – by then Henry Tang – was quoted as saying

> With hindsight, all parties concerned might have underestimated the complexity involved, and it was a very ambitious attempt in putting together the event within such a short time span. He did not observe any trace of irregularity in the organisation and implementation process.

Normal practice with minutes of a meeting is to show them in draft to the chairman first, then circulate to other attendees for comments once the chairman was content that they were an accurate reflection of what had been said and decided.

At the beginning of economic relaunch, the ERWG meetings were being held so close together that we did not have time to let the chairman see the draft first, rather we were circulating to all attendees in parallel. But for the 31 October meeting, the FS' Office made clear that they wished to revert to the normal practice.

On 7 November we received an email from a junior staff member which said in part

> As spoken, please let us have the draft minutes of the above meeting when they are ready, BEFORE circulating them to other members for comment.

Just to put the matter beyond any possible doubt, this was followed by an email from the FS' Administrative Assistant, the previously mentioned Shirley Yuen, dated 11 November requesting *inter alia*

> draft notes of ERWG meeting on 31 Oct (pl clear them with FS before circulation)

We of course had had no objection to this as it was merely a return to the normal practice and as ERWG meetings would from now on be much less frequent there was time for us to revert to it.

On 12 November the draft minutes were duly forwarded to FS' Office and on 14 November Yuen informed us that they had been cleared by the FS for circulation. The other members were then given their opportunity. At the end of this process, we had an agreed set of minutes seen and approved by all parties.

The differences between these and the original draft were very minor indeed. Most importantly, the key sentence "He did not observe any trace of irregularity in the organisation and implementation process" was still included. Copies of the agreed minutes were later to be given to the Audit Department and the Independent Commission Against Corruption.

On 16 August 2004, a junior in FS' Office had telephoned the note taker of the 31 October meeting, David Chiu of InvestHK, and asked that the key sentence be deleted. Chiu e-mailed back to the FS Office pointing out that the minutes had been circulated for comments in November of the previous year. As they were now agreed by all parties, such a substantive change could not be effected by a phone call.

The reply from the FS' office the same day said in part

> Thank you for your clarification. We might have missed the memo concerned last time, and would like to propose an amendment to the draft minutes please. Grateful if you could delete the sentence at paragraph 6 "He did not observe...".

At the ERWG meeting the next day, under item 1 dealing with "Confirmation of Minutes", the sentence was indeed deleted.

The effect of this recitation on the court was immediate and its significance understood. After all, it was clear from other evidence that in late July and early August 2004, CSB had been preparing the way for the disciplinary action against me and corresponding with Tang to clarify his position on various matters. Someone had obviously been reviewing past records and concluded that this sentence in the minutes was – how shall we put this delicately – "inconvenient".

The media in particular were electrified. In the Government, the agreed minutes of a meeting are sacrosanct. No-one can go back and change the record eight-and-a-half months later. The next day, all the print media included this aspect of the case in their report, most in moderate coverage, although Ming Pao (one of the more serious papers) gave it a full page with the sequence of e-mails highlighted.

THE SECOND DAY (25 February) saw Richard Gordon ploughing on to complete our case. Once again, one particular part of the argument caught the court's – and the media's – attention.

In an e-mail from me to Tang, I had stressed the need for a senior official to come out publically and make clear that HarbourFest had the full support of the Government. His reply e-mail began with the words "Stop dreaming." The print media, and Radio Television Hong Kong's English language channel played up this point in their coverage.

Day 3 saw Joe Fok on his feet to begin the Respondents' defence. He did not finish by close of play, so inevitably the reserve day had to be used.

Day 4 began rather unusually. Fok said that before resuming the arguments he had started to put forward the day before, he wished to clarify two matters that had attracted media coverage earlier in the proceedings. The first concerned the change to the agreed minutes of the 31 October meeting. He pointed out that the first item on the agenda of meetings almost invariably concerned the minutes of the previous meeting. This was the final opportunity to make sure the record was correct. The fact of the eight-and-a-half month delay was not in itself sinister, it was simply a reflection of the fact that there was a long interval before the next meeting.

The Respondents' argument on this was seriously flawed for the obvious reason that all parties had had an opportunity to comment on the draft minutes in November 2004 when their memories of the proceedings were still fresh.

Judge Hartmann was not fooled for one minute. He sat back sharply in his chair upon hearing the "innocent" explanation and burst out: "Mr Fok, it does not take a genius to see that this was political manoeuvring." He used the same expression twice more in the next few minutes.

This was dynamite and the reporters covering the case were on the edge of their seats. At the next break they rushed outside to agree among themselves a Cantonese equivalent of "political manoeuvring". From lunchtime onwards, it was the number two story on cable news (the go-ahead for the $60 billion bridge to Zhuhai and Macao was the lead) with a big cut-out of Judge Hartmann juxtaposed with one of Henry Tang. The next day the print media also played the story prominently.

If the first clarification was a PR disaster, Fok was to do no better with his second which concerned the "Stop Dreaming" e-mail of 15 October 2003. He said it needed to be seen in its full context as part of a chain of e-mails. He then read out extracts from some of them including virtually the entire text of its immediate predecessor (from myself to the Financial Secretary). The key phrase was in part a belated attempt by me to discover who was supposed to be the Minister for HarbourFest. I disguised the source of the query by saying "There are already mutterings in the media and elsewhere about 'who is the Minister for HarbourFest'". So the exhortation to "Stop Dreaming", seen in its full context, was a direct denial of the system of Ministerial Accountability.

One can only assume that a Government internal meeting the previous day had become concerned at the stream of negative publicity the case was generating, and wanted to offset it. Far from clarifying the situation and calming things down, the intervention had poured oil on troubled flames. Presumably the inquest on the Friday would not have been a happy gathering.

In court, Fok reverted to the legal arguments and took up the whole of the remainder of Thursday. The judge squeezed his Friday programme so that Fok could finish, and then Gordon could reply to the points made.

THE CASE WAS ADJOURNED later that Friday afternoon for the judge to consider his verdict. At dinner that night before Gordon flew back to the UK, I felt we had not obviously lost any of the ten or so arguments we had put forward, and on at least half of them I felt we had been the clear winner.

The judge indicated that while he would get started on the

judgement straight away, pressure of other work including a duty trip outside Hong Kong meant he would not be able to finish within March. But on return he would give the case priority as he realised it had been going on for a long time. Both we and the Government took this to mean a decision by the end of April. In the event, we did not get the judgement until 4 July – surely not a coincidence for a case involving the American Chamber!

WORD CAME THROUGH on 3 July that judgement would be delivered at 4pm the following day, and we should present ourselves at court to receive it.

There is apparently no hard and fast rule about the format at this point. While it was unlikely the judge would read out his whole ruling in open court, he might want to deliver a short précis or make some remarks. But there was no requirement for the judge to be involved at all, he could allow his clerk to hand out the ruling. The best we were able to find out before the day was that some judges did it one way, some another and sometimes the same judge would deliver the ruling in different ways in different cases.

So at 3.45pm my wife and I, accompanied by our solicitor, a couple of friends (one of whom was Liz Bosher) and about 50 members of the media were in the common area outside the courtroom whose lights were off and whose door was locked. It remained so until 4pm sharp when the door was suddenly unlocked from the inside (the lights were still off), the clerk emerged with a single copy of the judgement and a covering letter, sought and obtained my solicitor's signature to confirm receipt then disappeared back into the courtroom locking the door behind him.

Immediately my wife and I and the solicitor ducked into a nearby interview room and started to read the 80-page decision. Meanwhile outside we could see (the wall and door of the room were floor to ceiling clear glass) the press hopping up and down bursting to know the result, and trying to judge from our expressions which way it had gone. After about 15 minutes they could stand it no longer and one of them politely pushed open the door and asked about the verdict.

I replied "I think we've won." Indeed we had although it took another 15 minutes of speed reading to get to the key paragraphs at the end. They read:

> For the reasons given, I am satisfied that each of the three decisions described in paragraph 11 of this judgement must be quashed. There will be orders of *certiorari* to this effect.

> In respect of costs, bearing in mind that the applicant was successful in the great majority of the challenges made by him and was successful in having all three decisions quashed, I am satisfied that he is entitled to his costs. Costs are therefore awarded to him.

Game, set and match.

The full text of the judgement is worth reading and can be found on the Judiciary's website[1]. It includes, for example, some fairly sharp (implied) criticisms of the Inquiry Committee – "Another Inquiry Committee may well have come to a different conclusion – I may have done so" and "In a number of instances the logic employed may have been questionable and the evidential basis thin" – and also sets out why in a number of areas the disciplinary procedures the Government has followed for many years are simply unlawful.

The key arguments that caused the judge to find in our favour were three. The first concerned whether the Inquiry Committee had applied the appropriate standard of proof (as distinct from onus of proof which everyone accepted should rest on the prosecution). In paragraph 100 of his judgement, Mr Justice Hartmann wrote

> I have grave doubts that the Inquiry Committee understood and applied the correct standard. This failure, in my view, meant

that the Committee's report did not do justice to the applicant and could not, nor should it have been, relied upon by the Secretary for the Civil Service.

Indeed the judge thought this point so fundamental that this reason alone was sufficient to quash SCS' decision.

The second key issue was denial of legal representation. The Government's case was that it would only allow such representation in compelling and exceptional circumstances. The judge took the view that the guiding principle should be fairness. He certainly did not want to open the door to legal representation in discipline cases as a matter of course, making clear that he thought it should be allowed only rarely where fairness required it. He went on to say

> In all the circumstances, I am satisfied that the decision to deny the applicant legal representation, having regard to the exceptional circumstances of his case, may well have materially prejudiced him in the presentation of his case. In short, the decision denied him natural justice." [paragraph 141]

The third key issue concerned the dual role played by the Department of Justice which was advising the Civil Service Bureau at different stages throughout the disciplinary process. Here too the judge found in our favour. In respect of one aspect of our challenge he wrote

> For the reasons given, I have, albeit with reluctance, come to the determination that a fair-minded and informed observer, having considered the facts, would have concluded that there was a real possibility of bias on the part of (the DoJ officer) arising out of his dual advisory role [paragraph 168]

In respect of a second aspect, he wrote

As such, in my opinion, it was quite clearly a breach of the rule of fairness....." [paragraph 172]

Finally, there was a pretty straightforward argument as to whether or not the CE could lawfully delegate his powers to deal with appeals to anyone (in this case, the Chief Secretary). The Judge found that on a simple reading of the law, he could not.

BACK FOR A MOMENT to the late afternoon of 4 July 2008, five years almost to the day since ERWG had endorsed the HarbourFest sponsorship proposal.

It was time to meet the media. A group of us then descended to the lower ground floor where the court building gives access straight onto a walkway. As reporters and photographers clustered round, I made a short statement beginning with the words "Today's decision is a tremendous victory for the rule of law in Hong Kong."

After a brief period of answering questions, I returned to my office nearby. It was then that I learned that the electronic media had not been present for the statement because they had set up their cameras and microphones at the street level on the ground floor. There was nothing else for it, we had to scurry back and face the music again. I stepped up to the microphone bank and tried to remember the exact words I had used earlier: "Today's decision is a tremendous victory for the rule of law in Hong Kong."

Would the Government appeal? We could not forecast with certainty. Although the judgement was so clear and soundly based, and there was a consequent risk of having their noses rubbed in it, nonetheless there were potential implications that might almost oblige CSB and/or DoJ to go to a higher court. For example, could other defendants who had been denied legal representation seek to re-open their cases?

When I was asked by the media, I immediately batted this one back to the Government. I also reminded the media that though we had been successful in overturning the three major adverse decisions against me, we had not been successful on all of the legal grounds we had advanced. So we would need to consider whether we should appeal. Very much tongue in cheek I indicated I thought it unlikely unless the Government did first.

We did not get the Government decision for more than two months. Although the loser in such cases has one month to lodge an appeal after certain formal notices arising from the initial judgement have been served, in the legal world August does not exist so the one month would run until September. Finally on the last possible day, the Government said it would not be appealing.

WITHIN A SHORT PERIOD, all the penalties to which I had been subjected were reversed. The serious reprimand and caution as to future conduct were withdrawn, the salary deduction was reimbursed with interest.

And I could at last lay claim to my Certificate of 30 years Long and Meritorious Service, for which I had become eligible in 2004 but which had been withheld for four years while the discipline case was brought to a final conclusion.

And in the autumn of 2008, Judge Hartmann was promoted from the High Court to the Court of Appeal.

Implications for the Accountability System

UNDER THE SYSTEM of Ministerial Accountability introduced in July 2002, everything that the Government did was to be in pursuit of a specified Policy Objective for which there would be a clearly identified Minister. Civil servants would continue to identify problems or issues, set out various alternatives for addressing them with the pros and cons, and it would then be for the Ministers to take all major decisions and accept the political responsibility for them.

In effect, the new Ministers would be taking over what had hitherto been a key part of the job of the Administrative Service. Exactly how this new relationship between Administrative Officers and Ministers would pan out was not exactly clear at the time, and indeed is not much clearer seven years after the system was introduced. Several of the initial group of Ministers were drawn from the civil service, and when Donald Tsang began his "second" term – actually his first full 5-year term – in 2007 and reshuffled portfolios and personalities, he again drew heavily on the AO Grade for his new Ministers.

If this practice continues, i.e. if in future administrations some of the Ministers continue to be drawn from the civil service, then inevitably politics will seep down into the AO Grade and the political neutrality which the new system was supposed to deliver will be compromised.

One post presents a special situation, and that is the Secretary for the Civil Service. On the one hand, this is clearly a Ministerial position. On the other hand, an undertaking was given when the

Ministerial Accountability system was introduced that SCS would in future always be someone with a civil service background because the post also functions as head of the civil service. Such an undertaking was intended to reassure civil servants that their interests would always be protected. HarbourFest was to show how hollow this gesture was.

The Economic Relaunch programme arose when the new system was a little under a year old. At the macro level it was clear the Financial Secretary was the right Minister to take responsibility for the overall relaunch effort because it cut across the work of several different Ministers. SHA was responsible for boosting community morale, SES was responsible for reviving tourism, SCIT was responsible for reassuring the business sector, and so on.

Each then had to invent, or gather, ideas for specific projects that would achieve their policy objectives. The FS chaired ERWG, and these three Ministers plus SFST (whose job was to reassure financial markets and to advise on disposal of public funds) were all made members. SHA came up with ideas at the community level (dancing under the stars in a Wanchai street, a mass cycle ride in the New Territories, etc), SES with plans to boost tourism with a major marketing campaign to be implemented by the Tourism Board, SCIT with a plan for Hong Kong to host a major business conference (the Forbes Global CEO Conference would actually be held in 2004, but Steve Forbes – a long time admirer of Hong Kong – flew in to the SAR in late June 2003, within hours of the CDC travel advisory being lifted, to sign the sponsorship agreement with me in a high profile ceremony).

HARBOURFEST BROKE the mould because it came direct to ERWG from the American Chamber without having been specifically endorsed by any Minister on the way. Moreover, this omission – which was very obvious – was not addressed when the idea was first considered by ERWG on 2 July 2003.

How hard would it have been for Leung to say to one of the

Ministers present (three were actually in attendance) or represented (the fourth, SHA, was absent himself but some of the staff who reported to him were there): "OK, I want you to take on this one"? Or when it was suggested InvestHK should vet the budget for the event, should not Tang have queried why the investment promotion agency for which he had responsibility was being assigned to be involved in an entertainment event?

But in the heat of the moment neither of these things happened and InvestHK was simply asked to carry on.

There was a second opportunity to raise these points, and indeed some new ones, at the follow-up meeting on 12 July. Did no one consider possible side effects of the decision to sharply raise ticket prices? If they did, they kept very quiet. Was it expecting too much to look to Ma, with responsibility for public finances, to query why the Government was to be a "sponsor only" when it was providing nearly 90% of the budget?

WHAT IS CLEAR with the benefit of hindsight is that the Ministers got the HarbourFest decision wrong in two major respects (as well as a number of minor ones).

First and foremost, it was simply too ambitious an event costing too much money to implement satisfactorily with such a short lead time. And second, a sponsorship relationship was inappropriate given the scale – both in absolute and proportionate terms – of the Government financial commitment. So, a mistake had been made at the political level, but without an identified Minister to carry the political can.

But instead of admitting that the mistake was essentially theirs, the Ministers collectively decided that the major share of the blame should fall on the head of the civil servant who had implemented their flawed decision. And in doing so they were able to rely on support and assistance from one of their ministerial colleagues – the nominal head of the civil service, the Secretary for the Civil Service Joseph Wong.

SCS could of course partly explain his position because there had been three reports (Audit; the "Independent" Panel; PAC) pointing in the direction of disciplinary action.

But if he had studied those reports closely he would have noticed one glaring omission that they all had in common: there is not a single word in any of them about the new system of Ministerial Accountability. And in a sense, this is correct because when it came to HarbourFest, there was no one accountable at the political level.

It is this clear omission that makes the case of HarbourFest so unique. In fact there were two different omissions: the failure to have a Minister; and the failure of anyone who dealt with the case to address the point. In other cases of perceived Government error (the handling of SARS itself, national security legislation, etc) the relevant Minister had always been called to account. Yet in this case, there was literally No Minister.

Where was LegCo, where were the media, where were the academics and political commentators? Was the failure to query the lack of a Minister a bi-product of Antony Leung's resignation? Could there have been a feeling that since one Minister involved had already fallen on his sword (albeit for different reasons), the focus of the next phase of the blame game should fall elsewhere?

For an SCS who took seriously that part of his responsibility to protect the civil service from political shenanigans, it might have been a pretty obvious question to ask who the Minister was.

ONE CONSEQUENCE of HarbourFest may well be that the role of head of the civil service must be taken away from a political appointee and given to the most senior actual serving civil servant. This is the situation in the UK which is to some extent the model on which Hong Kong draws.

Role of Individuals

WHO WERE the major players in the HarbourFest saga and how did they acquit themselves?

Two groups emerge with their reputations enhanced. The first comprises the squad from AmCham that stepped forward on their own initiative to help Hong Kong in her hour of need. The economy was in danger of imploding with empty aircraft, empty hotels, deserted restaurants and so on. But the Americans were not content to sit around waiting for the Government to rescue them or for something to just turn up. In typical American fashion they rolled up their sleeves and prepared to rescue themselves, and the rest of us in the process.

Their idea was too ambitious, but the blame for not gently telling them this and coaxing them down to a more modest project should fall on the members of ERWG, including of course myself. Could I – should I – have poured a healthy dollop of cold water on the scheme when it was still at a preliminary stage?

What is particularly remarkable is that when the event began to attract criticism and the Government Ministers backed off, Amcham did not quit and say – as they might have done – "OK if you don't want us to do this, we'll stop".

Rather, the AmCham trio of Thompson, Denzel and Nierman plus the team they had assembled buckled down and kept going.

AND THEY DELIVERED a remarkable entertainment programme. For all its problems, HarbourFest remains one of the largest and best attended cultural events of its kind ever staged here or indeed elsewhere in Asia.

Even now, I am from time to time stopped in the street by complete strangers and told words to the effect "I don't care what anyone says, I thought HarbourFest was absolutely fabulous."

THE SECOND GROUP comprises all my colleagues at InvestHK. A tiny administrative team that had been staffed to support a $65 million p.a. department suddenly found itself with a two thirds bigger budget for its core investment promotion duties (because of the $40 million p.a. "temporary" additional funds for the five years 2003-4 to 2008-9) and saddled with an extraordinary $1 billion additional responsibility to be expended quickly to save Hong Kong's economy.

And when HarbourFest – which was not, of course, an InvestHK initiative – became the subject of controversy and our lift lobby filled at times on a daily basis with scores of reporters and flashing cameras, all the staff stoically braved the media melée and carried on with their jobs. The extra work and strain brought on by the audit scrutiny and ICAC investigation were also stoically borne.

I remember calling all the staff together at one point and putting it to them in stark terms. "Look, we didn't ask for the project but we were given it to do. Everyone else is abandoning AmCham. We could do so too if we wanted. But the fact is InvestHK was set up to support the international business community. If we run away from the biggest international chamber in its hour of need, we may as well wind up the whole department."

I promised to accept the responsibility on my own shoulders and to shield them as much as possible from the antics of the media. I thanked them for the many individual private messages of support I had received from them and said the best way they could help me was to attract as many new companies to set up in Hong Kong as possible. In other words, they should focus on our core business of investment promotion and not be distracted by the noise all around.

In the event the number of completed investment projects facilitated by InvestHK in 2003 was 142, the highest in our history up to that point and a 20% increase over 2002, despite the virtual loss of the second quarter.

NOT MANY THINGS about economic relaunch and HarbourFest still make me angry. But the failure of any senior person in the Government to thank the staff of InvestHK for their remarkable contribution to Hong Kong's well-being in 2003 leaves a bitter taste.

The contrast with the private sector could not have been more marked. The doyen of the Indian business community, Hari Harilela, invited the whole department to a buffet dinner at his own home when the controversy was at its height. He also made sure I sat on the head table for the annual Dhiwali dinner. The Italian Chamber insisted that I be Guest of Honour at a high profile fashion event that they knew would receive extensive media coverage. Many other international chambers made public gestures of support. The chairman of the British Chamber went on to give written evidence on my behalf in the disciplinary hearing itself.

THE PERFORMANCE of the Director of Audit Ben Tang was mixed. On the one hand he was new to the job, there obviously had to be an investigation of HarbourFest, and he did put his finger on the root cause of the problem: that sponsorship was not an appropriate form of financing a project where the Government was paying most of the bill. It is a pity that he did not then take that point to its logical conclusion and attribute many of the other weaknesses that he had identified as consequences of that initial flawed decision, rather than as stand-alone errors.

I was disappointed by the report by Moses Cheng and Brian Stevenson. It seemed to put about 50% of the blame on AmCham, 45% on me, and 5% on some unspecified group of others. While it could not ignore the part played by ERWG in endorsing the project at the outset, the report sought to shield the members from a proper share of the responsibility by saying that they had been inadequately supported by InvestHK at the assessment stage. If ERWG had wanted a more in-depth assessment, it had only to ask. Not surprisingly, some of the report's conclusions were faulty and some of the recommendations simply unworkable especially in an emergency situation. For example, the recommendation that finances should come from the private sector with the Government providing at most a minor part of the funding was simply pie in the sky in light of the circumstances prevailing in the middle of 2003. Similarly, the idea that payment of agreed sponsorship fees in stages should be regarded as loans fully reimbursable would mean no event organiser would ever work with the Government. The report's allegation of excessive fees being paid to some artists (but not the Rolling Stones, though that had been the original false news report that generated so much negative publicity) was based entirely on an unreliable website.

I took, and take, particular exception to the allegation that "DGIP and InvestHK traded due diligence for expediency in unjustifiably hiding behind a narrow interpretation of sponsorship." This implies that we invented an especially narrow interpretation just to apply to HarbourFest, which is completely false. We applied to HarbourFest exactly the same interpretation that we applied to every other event we sponsor.

THE MEMBERS of the Legislative Council, in particular those on the Public Accounts Committee, failed the people of Hong Kong: they were so excited at the prospect of a live human sacrifice that they forgot to ask the most obvious political question of all: who was the Government Minister responsible. While Audit and the "Independent" Panel were both guilty of the same sin of omission and should take some blame, they could at least argue that they had a narrower remit. But the failure by LegCo to even raise the subject is simply inexcusable: it is a fundamental part of their constitutional duty.

I cannot bring myself to dwell for too long on the members of the Inquiry Committee which conducted the disciplinary case. It seems likely that they simply buckled under the weight of public expectation bearing in mind that the Chief Executive had personally, on receipt of the report of the "Independent" Panel, publicly asked SCS to consider whether disciplinary action should be taken against any individual. And the Financial Secretary had turned up personally to give evidence for the prosecution. It was certainly odd that a committee chaired by an aspirant lawyer should have failed to adequately distinguish between two basic legal concepts such as burden of proof and standard of proof. And surely an engineer could have understood that when a 15-month project has to be delivered within 3 months, most of the elements of the Gantt chart (a bar chart used by engineers to show how a project is going to be taken from inception to completion through a number of overlapping or sequential development stages) are going to have to run in parallel instead of being sequential.

FORMER SECRETARY for the Civil Service Joseph Wong introduced and operated for many years a civil service disciplinary system now proven to be unlawful because it was so blatantly unjust. Therefore civil servants have not been treated fairly and the wider community interest has not been served. Throughout my own discipline case, there was a steady stream of one-sided leaks to the media which must have originated from within the Civil Service Bureau.

Since Mr Justice Hartmann's ruling, Wong has been quoted in the media as saying that his conscience was clear.

THE CAMEO APPEARANCE in the case by Chief Secretary Rafael Hui deserves at least a mention. Judging by the media reports, the appeal which I had submitted to the Chief Executive in October 2005 was delegated (unlawfully) to him in early 2006. Yet the decision to reject the appeal did not emerge until late January 2007.

It seems unlikely that the long lapse of time was taken up by a detailed examination of the merits of the appeal. It seems more likely that the file gathered dust in the "too difficult" tray on the CS's desk, and was only pulled out when the subject threatened to become an issue in the forthcoming CE election.

There was then a fascinating coda whereby some members of the press seemed to know the outcome of the appeal before I did. I doubt – in the absence of a properly constituted Commission of Inquiry, or LegCo Select Committee – that we will ever get to the bottom of the matter.

I HAVE DELIBERATELY left until last the evaluation of those who attended or were represented at the meetings of ERWG.

The civil servants present, whether as members or "in attendance" in support of their Ministers, generally (and quite naturally) limited their participation to matters directly touching on their own departments. The bulk of the serious discussion and deliberation was undertaken by the five Ministers (FS, SFST, SHA, SES and SCIT). None of them were to cover themselves with glory.

The Financial Secretary at the start of economic relaunch was Antony Leung. Basically he did a good job at the macro level, getting the broad thrust of the programme right, stimulating the generation of a large number and wide variety of ideas, and putting in place the machinery to execute them with the full support and assistance of InvestHK.

But he chaired the meeting of ERWG on 2 July which gave only cursory scrutiny to the AmCham proposal. He also chaired the meeting on 12 July which almost casually changed the ethos of the event and also severely circumscribed the Government's role in it by specifying that we were to be a "sponsor only". Had this not been done, had he for example said that in view of the scale (and proportion) of the Government contribution we should be a co-organiser, then there would inevitably have been a proper discussion about the appropriate department to take on this role. Many of the problems which subsequently emerged might have been avoided. AmCham would even have had an opportunity to reconsider its own involvement.

Perhaps Leung was distracted by other issues: just four days later, on 16 July, he resigned as the controversial "car purchase" case finally caught up with him. Suddenly the man who at one stage seemed the front runner to be the next Chief Executive was gone from the scene altogether.

Leung was succeeded after a brief interval of three weeks or so by Henry Tang moving up from the post of SCIT. In constitutional terms, Tang then inherited responsibility for everything – good or bad – which Leung had done. Much was very good, but in the case of HarbourFest, this was the equivalent of what rugby players call a "hospital pass". Whoever caught the ball was going to end up politically injured.

At this point, some of Tang's past actions and inactions began to catch up with him. As SCIT, he had agreed to the FS making one of his department heads the staff officer for economic relaunch, and the Controlling Officer for $1 billion. He had kept silent when the investment promotion agency for which he was responsible was given the task of checking the budget for an entertainment event, and subsequently being given the role of sponsor. He had pointed out that $100 million was a lot of money (hardly an insight) but had not completed the thought by querying the proposed role of "sponsor only".

And as SCIT, he had never considered himself as having political responsibility for the event. Had he done so, he would surely have sought to involve SHA.

Such a laid back stance almost amounts to abdication. And there were to be two consequences, one short term and one longer term. The immediate one was that when HarbourFest began to attract criticism there was no Minister to shield the FS – he was forced to front up in public and at LegCo himself because he had overall responsibility for relaunch. Longer term, there were even implications for the 2012 CE election. The media consider Tang a front runner, and some also see John Tsang (his successor as SCIT, and later also as FS) as a possible candidate. Had Tang clearly accepted responsibility for HarbourFest while he was SCIT, then it would have been Tsang who was forced to catch the hospital pass, probably doing enough damage to him politically to knock him out of the 2012 race altogether, assuming that he did wish to take part.

GIVEN THIS SEQUENCE of events, it is hard to blame John Tsang for completely ducking the HarbourFest issue when he took up the position of SCIT. He had not been in the relaunch/HarbourFest loop when all the key decisions had been made and by the time he became a member of ERWG the die had been cast.

The same cannot be said for the other three members of ERWG: Stephen Ip as SES, Patrick Ho as SHA, and Fred Ma as SFST. All had – or should have had – a role.

As Minister responsible for the tourism industry, one of the claimed target beneficiaries of HarbourFest, Ip must have known that the lead time for tourism marketing promotions to be effective (around 9 months) was simply incompatible with the lead time for the event (around 3 months). This was a strong argument in favour of a more modest project, but the argument was never articulated.

Ho as SHA was the Minister with responsibility for cultural and entertainment events, and he had a department (LCSD) directly under him which organised similar events. HarbourFest fell clearly within his remit, yet he somehow managed not to be engaged to any significant degree. The fact which should have been known to him, and possibly but not necessarily to other ERWG members, that a festival on this scale needed a very long lead time if it were to be successfully organised, was another powerful argument for a more modest event.

Once again, the silence of the Minister and his representatives meant the opportunity for an informed debate on this aspect was lost.

FINALLY, MA SAT silently by while $100 million was allocated on the basis that the Government would be a "sponsor only", instead of the organiser or co-organiser, of an entertainment event. His only significant involvement after the key ERWG meetings was to discuss informally with some LegCo Members whether to move a motion of reprimand (directed at me) in the full council by way of apology and as a means of showing the Government's regret.

One factor stands out from this roll call of less than brilliant administration: not one of the four main players (Leung, Tang, Ho and Ma) had ever been civil servants in the Administrative Service. Only the two bit players (John Tsang and Ip) were holdovers from the pre-Accountability System era.

Personal Reflections

NOT SURPRISINGLY, the whole economic relaunch exercise and in particular the HarbourFest event have left me with a torrent of emotions.

The eventual vindication in the High Court came too late to save my career which up to that point had been going well and exceeded my wildest expectations when I had joined the AO Grade back in 1980. One minute I was flying along in a Staff Grade A post (second highest level) and the job was going so well that even a further promotion to Staff Grade A+ (the highest level) seemed not out of the question. The next I was charged with Misconduct facing potential dismissal.

While the possible financial implications for my family were serious, it was the shame that brought me to the lowest point in morale terms. That I, who had joined the ICAC in 1974 as part of the first wave of new recruits (I had been a member of Induction Course 1A), I, who had stood shoulder to shoulder with two of the finest public servants in Hong Kong's history in Jack Cater and John Prendergast to fight the scourge of corruption in our community, should now stand charged with Misconduct – well, it just about broke my heart.

That feeling was compounded by the ICAC investigation of HarbourFest. The Financial Secretary's Office had referred the matter to the police when complaints of irregularity first surfaced. Meanwhile a former LegCo Member Tsang Kin Shing had very publicly made a complaint to the ICAC along the lines that "there must be corruption" even without any evidential basis whatsoever. The two law enforcement agencies had then agreed ICAC would take it on. I was duly interviewed – to soften the blow the investigators came to my office instead of inviting me to theirs – and a lot of the department's files were taken away.

Of course after the investigation I was completely cleared, as was everyone else associated with HarbourFest, and all the documents were returned. But the exercise left a bitter taste. It was no real consolation to me – well, perhaps it was just a little – when officers from the police Organised Crime and Triad Bureau interviewed me in December 2008 in connection with a report someone had made about the belated alteration to the ERWG minutes. Apparently the complaint was that this constituted conspiracy to pervert the course of justice. I could not resist a wry smile.

Yet in the depths of that despair, I found the strength to resist the injustice that some seemed determined to inflict upon me. In some ways, it was a reflection of the same spirit that had caused me to apply for the ICAC in the first place: you do not bow to the forces of darkness just because the perpetrators have all the wealth and power behind them. I hadn't acted that way in 1974 and I was damned if I would do so 30 years later in 2004 when I was first put on notice of the possibility of disciplinary charges.

So I set about systematically organising myself to fight the charges. I consulted with my family and received their total unequivocal support. The message from my in-laws was quite emphatic: you are not to worry about resources, you are to fight this case all the way up to the Court of Final Appeal if necessary (I learned something about Chiu Chow people – if you pick a fight with one, you'd better prepare to fight the whole tribe). I consulted a friend in the legal fraternity who had previously been a lawyer in the Government and through his introduction came to engage the solicitors firm of Herbert Smith. Then, as I explained earlier, when the request to be legally represented was (unlawfully) rejected, I sought the best alternative representation I could get in Christine Loh.

Finally, I resolved that in no circumstances would I allow the discipline case to distract me in any way from my performance as

Director-General of Investment Promotion. Hence the appeal to my colleagues in InvestHK to keep up their spirits and to keep up their good work. They responded magnificently. For my part, I kept up the backbreaking travel schedule that saw me clock up over one and a quarter million air miles in eight years. In speeches all over the world, I maintained my faith in, and support for, Hong Kong.

NOW TO THE CASE ITSELF. The first thing that needs to be said about the Hong Kong Government's disciplinary procedures is that they are blatantly one-sided and the odds are stacked against the accused officer. Once charged, the burden of proof in effect shifts to the defendant and it is virtually impossible to discharge that burden even when concrete evidence is produced to prove that the detailed charges, or at least significant elements of them, are simply wrong. The underlying philosophy is that you must be guilty because the Government has charged you. The Inquiry Committee's role is to work with the prosecutor to put a superficial coat of respectability on the proceedings. The best bet for the defendant is to plead guilty right away and then throw himself on the mercy of the "court". A suitable display of remorse should then secure a mild punishment. Woe betide the defendant who dares to claim innocence.

In the light of Mr Justice Hartmann's ruling, the Civil Service Bureau will need to make a number of significant changes to the present procedures. I am sure they will do (at least) the minimum necessary to comply with the law. I wish I could be equally sure that the underlying philosophy would undergo a similar sea change to bring about a spirit of fairness. The auguries are not encouraging. In later correspondence dealing with the issue of costs (of which more later) CSB wrote "Nor does it (i.e. CSB) accept the question of 'fairness' should come into play in these issues."

The practical arrangements for the hearing could also use a major overhaul. The primitive system of recording the proceedings on tape, but not attempting to provide a written record – indeed, refusing permission for a stenographer to be present even at the defendant's expense – is an invitation to injustice. I lost count of the many hours I was forced to spend on weekends, public holidays, early mornings, late evenings, crouched over a tape recorder trying to turn almost inaudible tapes into a semi-respectable transcript. When my career was at stake, there were no resources. When a political objective was at stake (the "Independent" Panel), money was no object.

Mention of work brings me back to another point. Reading the various reports on the case (Audit, Panel, PAC, Inquiry Committee), both at the time they came out in 2004 and 2005, and again in 2009 when writing this book, I could not escape the feeling that there must be a second DGIP somewhere. After all, I knew I had a full time job running a small but important Government department. That job required extensive overseas travel for around a quarter of my time, requiring Hong Kong duties to be compressed into the balance of time actually spent here. Almost continuous jetlag had to be coped with. The additional assignment of what became known as AsiaWorld-Expo had to be handled. The whole support role for economic relaunch had to be managed on a part-time basis on top of our regular duties, and our department even undertook a number of additional direct assignments here also, including sponsorship of the Liverpool and Real Madrid football matches.

All of this amounted to more than a full time job for one person. But from reading the reports there was clearly this other guy with time on his hands. He had the capacity to work almost full-time on HarbourFest, watching how AmCham spent every dollar, monitoring on a daily basis how many free tickets were given away for marketing purposes and to whom, ensuring that frequent budget revisions were prepared (by whom?) and scrutinised, etc., etc. I really wish there had been such a person: I could have used the help.

BUT ECONOMIC RELAUNCH and the disciplinary case also had their lighter moments. At one stage it looked as though Liverpool would back out of the football match here because of health concerns: then manager Gerard Houlier had had a heart problem and operation, and was nervous about coming to Hong Kong while SARS was still in the air. The event organiser gave me his telephone number (he was at home in France on holiday) and I talked to him. When Houlier said he would take advice from his doctor, I asked for and was given the contact number for him as well. So at 9pm one night, I was sitting in my office talking to Houlier's doctor persuading him that it would be safe for the team and manager to visit. He at the time was on the touchline of a training session for an England youth team, so the conversation was frequently interrupted as players came off the pitch. Messy, but it worked. I gave him contact details of the relevant medical professionals in Hong Kong and whether or not he actually got in touch with them (to this day I do not know) he felt reassured enough to advise Houlier that it was safe to come.

Another memorable scene was a lunch at the Hong Kong Club on 4 July 2008 itself, when we were all waiting for the Judge's verdict scheduled for later that afternoon. Also present were Denise Yue (who had taken over from Joseph Wong as SCS) and Ian Wingfield from the Department of Justice who had advised CSB throughout my disciplinary proceedings. I made a point of approaching Yue and shaking her hand, and mentioned the afternoon date with destiny.

She asked me if I had a line to take ready. I replied that I had two, one for if we won and another for if we lost. She couldn't help bursting out laughing and said "So have we!", before going on to suggest that we swapped versions. By chance (seating is by drawing lots) I found myself close to Wingfield for the meal. "Actually," he said "There are only two possible lines to take. One is 'Over the Moon'; the other is 'Sick as a Parrot'." Around 5pm that day after the verdict was out, he had the grace to send me an e-mail entitled "Sick as a Parrot".

I HAVE BEEN ASKED at various times whether or not I think there was an element of racism in the decision to bring charges against the only non-ethnic Chinese member of ERWG. My answer has always been the same. While there were undoubtedly some individuals involved in the case who have racist tendencies, I do not believe the Administration has an institutional bias on the grounds of race. It is far more likely that I got the blame because I was the only person not at the key meetings.

HarbourFest and the discipline case also had some positive messages about Hong Kong. After all, eventually justice did prevail. And where else in the world would a head of department under discipline have been allowed to carry on with his duties while taking his employer to court?

Lurking in the background to the whole story of HarbourFest and the discipline case is my relationship with the man who is now our Chief Executive, Donald Tsang. It is widely known that he and I have in the past worked closely together and been friends. When I joined the Government in 1980 he was the head of the small team which looked after Administrative Officers, so he was actually the first person I met on my first day. Later our paths had crossed a number of times: we worked together in Finance Branch on things like the Defence Costs Agreement, financing the airport railway, the transition budget and so on. I also wrote a number of speeches for him including the famous (or should that be notorious) "Silence of the Lambs". Later when he was elevated to Financial Secretary I became the first head of the Business & Services Promotion Unit which was part of his office. We worked together on a number of projects, most notably the negotiations which led to Hong Kong Disneyland.

In 2003, Tsang's own position in the Government was not particularly strong. It was no secret that then Chief Executive Tung Chee Hwa preferred Financial Secretary Antony Leung. Hence when SARS struck, Tsang was given the job of sweeping the back lanes while Leung was given the much more glamorous job of restoring community morale and reviving the economy. The screenplay came unstuck when the car purchase scandal forced Leung's resignation in mid-July. Tang then took over as FS and favourite son. But as a relative newcomer to ministerial position, he was not ready to take over when Tung was forced to quit in the spring of 2005 as the credibility of his Administration dribbled away. But that was to come later. In 2003 and 2004, the local media saw every issue in terms of the race between Tsang and Tang for the 2012 CE election. Even my discipline case was interpreted in this context. There is an expression in Cantonese which roughly translates as "Shooting the horse to kill the jockey." Because of the perceived closeness of Tsang and myself, there was speculation that the case against me was being pursued to weaken him (and also to show that he was too weak to protect "his own man").

I had foreseen this problem at an early stage. Accordingly, I went to see Tsang at his official residence (Victoria House) one Saturday morning in December 2003 after making sure by phone that he was home and free to meet. For some reason we both felt more comfortable discussing the matter in the garden rather than indoors. "It's going to get very nasty," I told him, referring to the HarbourFest saga. "But whatever happens you must stay clear of it. You will only be weakened by it. Don't get involved and don't try to help. I'm big enough and ugly enough to take care of myself. Hong Kong needs you for more important things." At the time these words seemed rather pretentious – and looking at them again now they still seem so. But as it happened they turned out to be prescient.

Tsang only took up the post of Chief Executive in 2005, by which time the discipline case was already over. But that did mean he had to receive the appeal. Because of our past relationship he decided it would be better not to deal with the appeal himself, and instead delegated to the Chief Secretary. Though no doubt well intentioned, the act of delegation was itself unlawful.

In early 2009, when I belatedly received my 30 Years Long and Meritorious Certificate from SCS (due in 2004 but withheld because of the discipline case) as I stepped down from the stage Tsang shouted from the front row of the audience "Stop suing us!" to which I instantly replied "Well pay up then." This was a reference to the fact that in December 2008 I had petitioned him again, this time on the question of costs. The total amount of money I had to spend to clear my name was over $6 million, but I was advised that despite the costs order by the judge I was likely to get back much less because legal fees arising during the discipline stage, and other costs, were not covered by the order. The total shortfall is likely to exceed $3 million.

Thus the penalty for being found guilty of mishandling $100 million of public money was around one month's salary, whereas the penalty for being found innocent was more than one year's salary. This, I argued, was unfair. I appealed for a full reimbursement but without any element of compensation for the years of stress and loss of career. In April 2009, after taking advice from the Department of Justice and CSB, Tsang rejected my appeal. He was apparently impressed by the argument that there was no precedent for reimbursing legal fees incurred during a discipline case. (It is hard to see how there could have been a precedent, since SCS had always rejected requests by defendants to be legally represented!) More impressed by that argument, anyway, than by my argument for fair treatment. No doubt the decision was politically expedient. But it was not the right decision that an AO would have taken in the old days. So the jockey had survived the ordeal and was still alive and well, but the horse had incurred a $3 million injury and should be put down.

Many well-meaning people, from inside and outside the civil service, have encouraged me to sue for compensation. After all, the key adverse decisions against me have all been found to be illegal, I definitely have suffered in terms of career, health, etc. And it is certainly tempting to try to reclaim at least the amount the case has cost me, plus a suitable margin to cover time and trouble. Unfortunately, under the Common Law system it is not enough to show that the Government has made mistakes and that as a consequence you have suffered loss. Rather to have any chance of success you have to show that the wrong decisions were motivated by malice. The circumstances of HarbourFest and the disciplinary case which resulted, and in particular some of the aspects of the way the case was conducted, can give rise to suspicion of certain peoples' *bona fides*. But that is some way short of proving malice. So this option can only be pursued if further information comes to light.

ALL THROUGH MY CAREER as an AO, one thing had been impressed upon me by senior colleagues, including in particular by Tsang himself. Behind closed doors, there should be the most vigorous examination of every proposal. All the pros and cons should be set out, examined and discussed. No officer, however junior, should feel inhibited from expressing reservations about any idea floated by even the most senior person present. But once a decision had been reached – once there was a "company position" – then everyone involved was expected to stand by that decision, and support and defend it as necessary. Tsang has been especially keen on this formula. I have seen him, both as Secretary for the Treasury and as Financial Secretary, be very democratic at the discussion stage, even allowing his own proposals to be shot down. But once there has been a conclusion, he requires everyone involved to back it 100%.

In the case of HarbourFest, I played by these old rules. I only realised too late in the process that the old system had broken down, at least temporarily. It emerged that at the ERWG meetings at which I was not present there had been no in-depth discussion of the various alternatives behind closed doors. There had simply been a proposal, a presentation to explain it, and at most cursory consideration.

Did none of the civil servants attending spot the flaws? Or did they simply defer to the obvious enthusiasm of their political masters? Presumably the Ministers attending thought the time devoted to considering the project was adequate in the circumstances prevailing. And when controversy arose, instead of standing together to explain and defend their original decision, all those persons who had been present tried their best to avoid taking responsibility and leave it to the one person who had not been there to carry the can.

The message this sent to the civil service was very clear: in a crisis, the Ministers will desert you as they rush to escape from the political heat. My senior civil servant colleagues – whether or not they liked me personally, and I realise quite a few do not – were seriously worried. As a consequence, the Administrative Service Association took the (as far as I know unprecedented) step of petitioning the Secretary for the Civil Service not to proceed with disciplinary action against me. Their concern obviously was whether the old system of collective responsibility had broken down, and if it had, what was to replace it. In the bunfight which the political climate now required, would civil servants in future be sacrificed as a matter of course? Did the new system of "Ministerial Accountability" mean that when things went wrong the Ministers would meet to decide which civil servant would be held accountable? Their worries would not have been eased by SCS' response. He, having once been an AO but lately converted to Minister, decided his bread was buttered on the other side now and ignored the petition.

There is a wonderful expression in Cantonese to the effect "Do less, do less wrong. Do nothing, do nothing wrong." Those in the civil service who took this as the safest operational mode for a successful career were strengthened in their resolve. I have never been able to live by this mediocre philosophy, and I like to think that most of my AO colleagues feel similarly. But the writing is on the wall.

THE QUESTION NOW is whether HarbourFest was a one-off aberration or establishes a pattern that will be repeated in future. Perhaps it was not a coincidence that four of the six Ministers involved had never been Administrative Officers. The official line that civil servants and Ministers work together as one united team will ring hollow if there are further cases. As a precaution in the interim, any prudent civil servant will have to take steps to ensure that anything he is asked to do is clearly in support of an identified policy objective for which there is an identified Minister. Moreover, he will need also to spell out in writing the cons as well as the pros of all possible courses of action to ensure that the Minister cannot later claim to have been unaware of downside risks. And at the first sign something is going not quite to plan, the Minister will have to be alerted. This will undoubtedly slow down administration generally and the policy making process in particular, but to do otherwise would leave the civil servant unfairly exposed. And how a future emergency could be coped with is unclear. But such is the legacy of HarbourFest and the discipline case.

STRANGELY ENOUGH, I was quite prepared to be the public face of blame for the mis-steps in HarbourFest. After all, someone had to take it on the chin and I was nearest when the bomb went off. As far as I was concerned, it was part of the job. But when to protect themselves and their political prospects some people took the process a stage further and launched disciplinary action, there was only one thing I could say.

No, Minister.

Notes

Political Backdrop

[1] Leung resigned with effect from 16 July 2003.

[2] Tung's U.S. holdings were disclosed in his Declaration of Interests.

Outbreak of SARS

[1] The currency used throughout this book is the Hong Kong dollar (HK$), which since 1983 has been pegged to the US$ at a rate of 7.8:1.

Public Accounts Committee

[1] Since this episode, Li has stepped down from the Legislative Council and has reverted full-time to his accountancy occupation including acting as Independent Non-Executive Director of listed companies, such as Meadville Holdings Ltd.

HarbourFest: The Event

[1] All South China Morning Post headlines.

[2] As advised at the time by sources in the entertainment industry.

Judicial Review

[1] *www.judiciary.gov.hk*; the case reference is HCAL 41/2007

Acknowledgements

I SHOULD BEGIN by giving thanks for Hong Kong's legal system, and the robust independence of our Judiciary, without which a gross injustice could not have been overturned. I should also thank the Hong Kong University for Science and Technology for providing me with space on a beautiful and serene campus which allowed me to focus on writing the book, and also providing an opportunity for me to work with our young people thereby serving the community after retirement.

As regards individuals, first should be Christine Loh whose strong and unequivocal support helped to sustain my morale in the fight. Hong Kong will know that it has matured politically when we have a Chief Executive with the courage and wisdom to appoint her as Minister for the Environment.

I should also like to thank Mark and Hester at Herbert Smith for all their hard work, and for their introduction to Richard Gordon QC. All three were not only utterly professional in their help, but also passionate in my defence. It would be remiss of me not to pay tribute to Jim Thompson, truly a gentleman and one of Hong Kong's great heroes.

Throughout the trials and tribulations of the past six years, my immediate and extended family have been unwavering in their support; in particular my wife Fanny, who gallantly escorted me to no fewer than seven concerts notwithstanding the media frenzy that arose each time we stepped out of the taxi.

I should like to thank the many people still in the Administration who have rendered me their quiet backing. Some would prefer to remain anonymous so I will name none. But suffice to say I will never forget all your efforts which have contributed so much to a happy outcome. And finally a word of appreciation to my editor Peter Gordon for keeping me, if not exactly on the straight and narrow, at least in sight of it.

MIKE ROWSE first came to Hong Kong in 1972 and has lived there ever since. After brief spells as a tutor and a tabloid journalist, he joined the Independent Commission Against Corruption on its establishment in 1974. After working in both the Operations and Corruption Prevention Departments, he joined the Government proper in 1980 as an Administrative Officer.

After a variety of different postings, Mike became the first Director of the Financial Secretary's Office from 1997 – 2000, and from 1999 – 2000 was appointed concurrently as the first Commissioner for Tourism. In those twin capacities, he was the lead negotiator with the Walt Disney Company which resulted in the building of Hong Kong Disneyland. In July 2000, Mike set up Invest HK, the investment promotion agency established by the Hong Kong Government, and was its first Director-General up to his retirement in December 2008. The agency won several awards during his tenure and was recently recognized as the best investment promotion agency in Asia.

In 2001 he became the first expatriate civil servant in Hong Kong's history to naturalise as a Chinese citizen.

Mike is married to Fanny Wong, former Political Editor of the South China Morning Post, and now a communications consultant. They have one daughter and one son. Mike also has two adult sons from a previous marriage.

A note on the cartoons

The other big story in 2003 was the "Yuen Long crocodile", evidently a released pet, which found a new home in the New Territories where it grew to a substantial size.

For many weeks, and to the glee of the Hong Kong public, it evaded the best efforts of the Government and the world's leading crocodile catchers. Pui-pui, as it was named after a competition, was finally apprehended and ultimately found a new home in the Hong Kong Wetland Park.

China's first manned-space launch was on 15 October 2003, carrying

the now celebrated Yang Liwei into orbit and became, not surprisingly, a subject of considerable local comment.

Gavin Coates is one of Hong Kong's best-known and prolific political cartoonists. The author and HarbourFest provided him with some of his best material.